The Power of IT

Also available from ASQC Quality Press

Information Service Excellence Through TQM: Building Partnerships for Business Process Reengineering and Continuous Improvement
Timothy Braithwaite

Small Business Success Through TQM: Practical Methods to Improve Your Organization's Performance
Terry Ehresman

Team Fitness: A How-To Manual for Building a Winning Work Team
Meg Hartzler and Jane E. Henry, Ph.D.

Business Process Benchmarking: Finding and Implementing Best Practices
Robert C. Camp

The Change Agents' Handbook: A Survival Guide for Quality Improvement Champions
David W. Hutton

Managing Finance for Quality: Bottom-Line Results from Top-Level Commitment
James A. F. Stoner and Frank M. Werner

To request a complimentary catalog of publications, call 800-248-1946.

The Power of IT

Maximizing Your Technology Investments

Timothy Braithwaite

ASQC Quality Press
Milwaukee, Wisconsin

The Power of IT: Maximizing Your Technology Investments
Timothy Braithwaite

Library of Congress Cataloging-in-Publication Data
Braithwaite, Timothy, 1942–
The power of IT: maximizing your technology investments / Timothy Braithwaite.
p. cm.
Includes bibliographical references and index.
ISBN 0-87389-349-2 (acid-free paper)
1. Information technology—Management. 2. Information resources management. I. Title.
HD30.2.B72 1996
658.4'038—dc20 95-42809
CIP

© 1996 by ASQC

All rights reserved. No part of this book may be reproduced in any form or by any means, electronic, mechanical, photocopying, recording, or otherwise, without the prior written permission of the publisher.

10 9 8 7 6 5 4 3 2 1

ISBN 0-87389-349-2

Acquisitions Editor: Susan Westergard
Project Editor: Kelley Cardinal

ASQC Mission: To facilitate continuous improvement and increase customer satisfaction by identifying, communicating, and promoting the use of quality principles, concepts, and technologies; and thereby be recognized throughout the world as the leading authority on, and champion for, quality.

Attention: Schools and Corporations
ASQC Quality Press books, audiotapes, videotapes, and software are available at quantity discounts with bulk purchases for business, educational, or instructional use. For information, please contact ASQC Quality Press at 800-248-1946, or write to ASQC Quality Press, P.O. Box 3005, Milwaukee, WI 53201-3005.

For a free copy of the ASQC Quality Press Publications Catalog, including ASQC membership information, call 800-248-1946.

Printed in the United States of America

 Printed on acid-free paper

ASQC
Quality Press
611 East Wisconsin Avenue
Milwaukee, Wisconsin 53202

Contents

Preface

This book is intended as an aid to business managers as they strive to successfully use information technology (IT) to make their companies more profitable. It is written from my perspective as an IT analyst and manager with over 30 years experience in applying computer technology to both government and business. To realize the power of IT one must understand the limitations as well as the capabilities of computers; that the exercise of discipline in systems development is essential; and that systems to better serve customers are possible only if they better serve employees first.

In the 1970s, I had the good fortune to work as a consultant/instructor for the Department of Defense Computer Institute in Washington, D.C. The Institute, specially created by the Office of the Secretary of Defense, had a unique mission regarding the fledgling use of computers in government. Its assignment was to familiarize senior officials (that is, general and flag officers as well as equivalent civilian agency executives) with not only the capabilities of computers, but also their limitations. It had become clear, even in the early days of computing, that a productive use of this new technology could only be realized after the in-depth analysis of the work task to be automated; and that this analysis had to be accomplished in full recognition of the limitations associated with the technology. The principal limitations were twofold: (1) Computers correctly accomplish only what they are properly instructed to accomplish; and (2) Their application must be appropriately subordinate to the human element controlling the work task.

This philosophy of the Institute identified many early concerns with the use and management of computers. This resulted in pioneering work in the areas of computer and communications security, data privacy and confidentiality, computer system acquisition, software development, and project management. Each of these problematic areas surfaced because of inherent limitations in computers, their application, and their manufacture, programming, integration, and operation in the workplace. Without knowledge of, and sensitivity to these limitations, decisions concerning the use of computers could not be intelligently made. Without such knowledge, officials would have only the "rosy" projections of computer technology advocates to guide them. (This usually means that given enough money and time, even the most exaggerated claims and promises can be made to work.) A more conservative approach was needed then and a more conservative approach is needed today.

In my first years after leaving the Institute, I heard few discussions concerning the limitations of computing. When the topic was brought up it was usually part of a postmortem of some disastrous attempt at automation. This failure to recognize and discuss such limitations, as a balance to all the exciting and glamorously advertised capabilities, put the decision-maker at a disadvantage. But then in the late 1980s American business was introduced to total quality management (TQM). With its emphasis on process, TQM legitimized the search for limitations in all aspects of business as part of the continuous quality improvement mandate brought on by global competition. It was now fashionable to seek out limitations and problems in the business' work processes, and this included the use of computers. My book, *Information Service Excellence Through TQM* (ASQC Quality Press, 1994), sought to assist information service organizations in their application of quality management principles to the business of building automated systems. Even though I was not a practicing quality management consultant, I thought that sharing my experiences while implementing TQM in three IT companies (from a senior staff position) would be helpful to other IT managers.

This book is directed to those business managers who are more frequently making far-reaching, expensive, and high-impact decisions concerning the technological path their company should take in a desire to remain competitive and profitable. These business managers are generally nontechnical by training, but are expected daily to not only run a business, but also to learn a technology that even computer professionals find difficult.

This book is directed primarily to the small to medium-sized business; those that can undoubtedly use IT to advantage, but are not large enough to have full-time personnel on staff to analyze such issues. Neither are these organizations large enough to generally consider contracting out such analysis to the big-name independent system houses or accounting firms.

Faced with such situations, managers have few choices for dealing with the technological decisions affecting the business. None of these are really acceptable.

- Managers can trust to luck that an application of technology within the business will succeed. With basic word processing and stand-alone spreadsheets/accounting operations, this may be possible. But as the complexity of IT applications increases, so does the business' dependence on those applications. Trusting the future of a business to luck becomes a risky proposition.

- Managers can trust that the information technologies presented in advertising and marketing materials will perform as claimed. It must be noted, however, that such materials and their claims are very high level and never address how such technologies will function within the day-to-day specifics of a workplace. These are technologies that may or may not solve problems or improve business activities yet to be analyzed. Trusting marketing and advertising materials alone will often lead to IT decisions being made on price alone. This is another risky proposition when dealing with an industry beset by price wars and the unrelenting demand to get new, supposedly better, faster, and cheaper products into the hands of the sales force.

• Lastly, managers can engage an independent consultant or local systems integration company for assistance. While this approach is preferable to the other two, the issues of competence, motivation, and contractual recourse are raised. Is the consultant or systems company truly competent to perform the required analysis and propose and manage the implementation of a feasible solution? How do you know? Is the consultant interested in your long-term welfare and business success or only its own short-term bottom line? How can you protect yourself contractually against failure of any systems provider to deliver and the potential subsequent loss of revenue should your business be interrupted? Also, how would you evaluate the quality claims of the systems provider? Since quality and value seem to be central to everyone's marketing brochure, how can managers separate fact from fiction?

This issue of quality and value should, in fact, be the key considerations for business managers when making IT decisions. Since quality of hardware, software, analysis, and support services, evaluated separately and in combination, represent the best predictor of project success and ultimate value, the quality management practices of each supplier and provider become the critical criteria for examination. If it can be determined that each systems supplier or provider is managing its business and hardware, software, and service delivery according to sound systems and quality management principles, then the chances of success, for any IT project, are substantially greater than if unsound system practices are being followed and quality principles are ignored.

The various quality management thought systems stress that the quality of any product or service is primarily determined by whether or not the process used to develop and deliver the product or service promotes quality. This is the standard used in this book.

Affixing the appearance of quality onto a product or service just prior to delivery usually has no lasting effect on reputation and is excessively expensive compared to building quality into a product or service. Also, attempts to correct quality deficiencies after the product is in the customers' hands is, without doubt, the most expensive course of action and threatens the very relationship between providers and customers.

But, how can business managers make such determinations concerning the myriad procedures and activities associated with an IT project? How, without becoming technical experts, can such judgments be made?

The answer, explored in this book, is to initially and then continuously evaluate the quality management practices of your systems provider during progression of an IT project, from early discussions of requirements through development, until system delivery and its operation in the workplace. After more than a decade of experience with the philosophies and principles of quality management, it is well known how to use them to evaluate the quality of any provider's manufacturing, development, assembly, or service delivery process, and to make a judgment concerning final product quality. In this case, the product is a functioning IT system that contributes value to a business.

This book seeks to assist business managers evaluate the quality awareness and practices of potential IT providers. The book presents a familiar and easily understood model that could be used to communicate with individuals and companies from the world of IT. Using this model can set your next technology project on a successful path and assist in keeping it there. The book provides some insights to help understand the highly complex world of today's technology. These focus on the analytic thought process that must be adhered to in bringing IT to your business. Finally, this book helps to remove the intimidation factor often experienced by less-technical managers when dealing with technologists; while at the same time helping managers realize that failure to be actively involved can be dangerous. Involvement is required. This book helps to facilitate that involvement.

Timothy Braithwaite
10961 Trotting Ridge Way
Columbia, MD 21044
410-997-0069

CHAPTER 1

Introduction

The purpose of this book is to provide business managers with information and a methodology for obtaining the best possible quality and value for their information technology (IT) dollar. The primary audience is business managers whose principal responsibilities are to administer the revenue-generating activities of the business. These responsibilities may also involve hardware and software management or other forms of information processing technology.

Hopefully, the information and methods presented here will be equally valid 10 or 20 years from now as they are today; for they deal with the thought process and human relations aspect of defining, developing, constructing, delivering, and successfully living with information technology in the workplace. Because of this, the book *will not* endeavor to argue merits or disadvantages of technologies that are in vogue today. It is assumed that the challenge of proper work division, shown in Figure 1.1, will be valid in the future and that the purpose of information systems development will still be to augment the strengths of people with the strengths of computer systems. While seeming to be fundamental, the potential for a misassignment of tasks between people and computers in poorly designed systems may be at the bottom of much of the dissatisfaction with IT when viewed from the employees' perspective (Figure 1.2). This figure illustrates the impact of IT systems on organizations, and

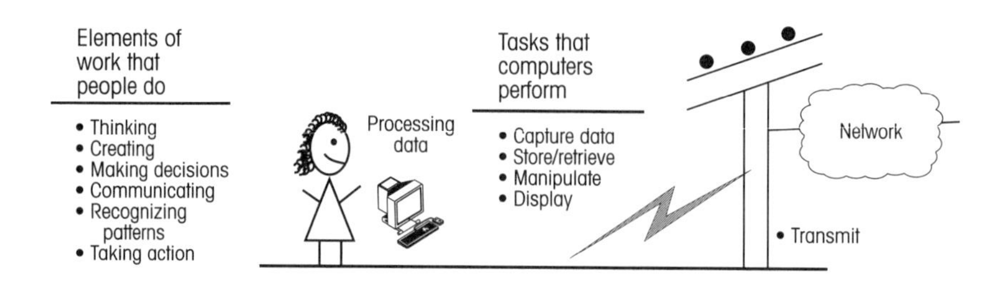

Figure 1.1. Division of work between people and computers.

whether or not, from the viewpoint of employees working with those systems, the impact was a success, a marginal success, or a failure. This perspective is crucial to the future of a business especially if senior management believes that IT should only enhance employees' job performance. Business managers must have a way to influence and evaluate the potential uses of technology, so that the business' overall effectiveness does not suffer from technology's misapplication. This book provides an approach to ensure that this evaluation activity is performed and that all aspects of the business process within the workplace are examined in sufficient detail to allow for the smooth implementation of technology systems.

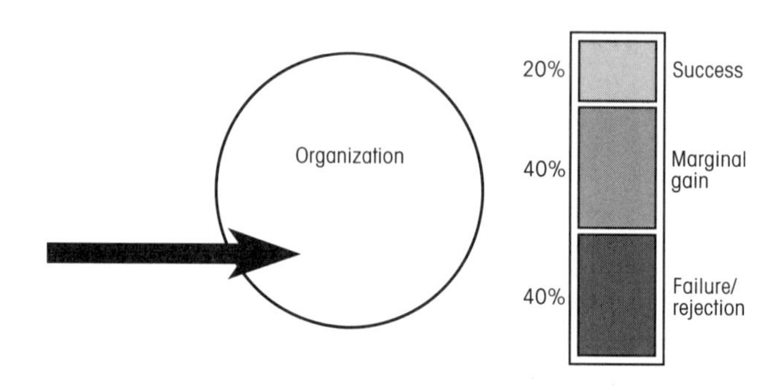

Source: Adapted from Ken Eason, *Information Technology and Organizational Change* (London: Taylor & Francis, 1988).

Figure 1.2. Success rates in information technology application.

Figure 1.3 portrays social and technical elements of a work process that must be taken into account during an attempt to apply IT to the business activity. The elements found in the left segment of the figure are the province of information technologists, while in the right segment are found those activities required to prepare the workplace for technical systems. The central segment identifies those activities needed to link the technical systems with the workplace and specifies the computer/people division of labor required of Figure 1.1. Historically, the fundamental problem of system design is that the left and right segments have not been treated as closely related. One goal of this book is to bring these two segments together by improving business managers' understanding of how to apply IT to a work process and by reminding information technologists of their reason for existence—the delivery of quality information systems that add value to the business.

As IT options multiply, it becomes more difficult for nontechnical business managers to converse with technologists except through the

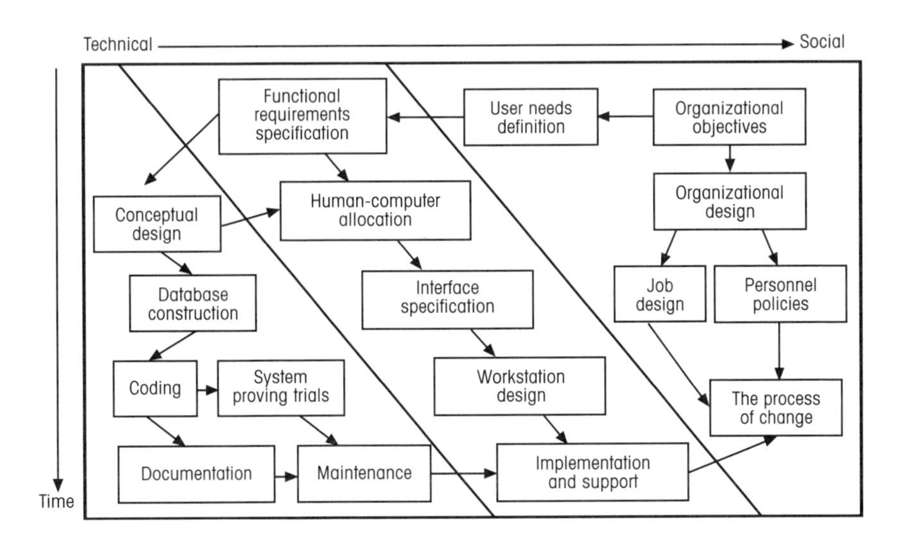

Source: Adapted from Ken Eason, *Information Technology and Organizational Change* (London: Taylor & Francis, 1988).

Figure 1.3. Social and technical elements of work process.

intermediary of systems analysts. For purposes of this book, a systems analyst is defined as one trained and skilled in the judicious application of IT components to the problems and added-value opportunities facing businesses. IT components include hardware, software, and communications. Judicious use of these components means that analysts are pushing no particular hardware or software solution, but rather are concentrating on the problem or added-value opportunity facing the business. It also means that the analysts are endeavoring to formulate, from available technology, the best possible solutions given prevailing constraints. To do this, the systems analysts must approach each job in a disciplined manner. This is known as the systems development process (SDP). It is accepted as the fundamental work process of system developers; is taught in all university programs; and is available in various commercially marketed versions. Figure 1.4 illustrates the steps or phases of a generic SDP. Whether performed manually or automatically, it is the thought process that is important. It resembles classical problem solving, and its phases cannot be circumvented if quality and value are to result. It is the way of rationale thinking when faced with problems, added-value opportunities, and/or alternative courses of action, each of which possess some degree of benefit and risk. It is a thought process that *must be* exercised when dealing with the complexities of using IT to solve business problems or benefit from opportunities.

The book is directed to business managers, in an attempt to level the playing field and give them increased abilities and confidence when dealing with in-house or out-of-house automated information systems and service providers. In the Baltimore/Washington, D.C., area there is a clothier by the name of Sy Sims, and he says, "Our best customer is an educated consumer." Many information systems professionals would echo this sentiment because they realize that truly successful applications of IT result from partnership—a partnership with nontechnical personnel that must exist on many levels to ensure that the tools of hardware, software, and information management are properly brought to bear on the business problem or added-value opportunity facing the organization.

In nontechnical language, this book addresses the roles and responsibilities of the members to that partnership. This text identifies what

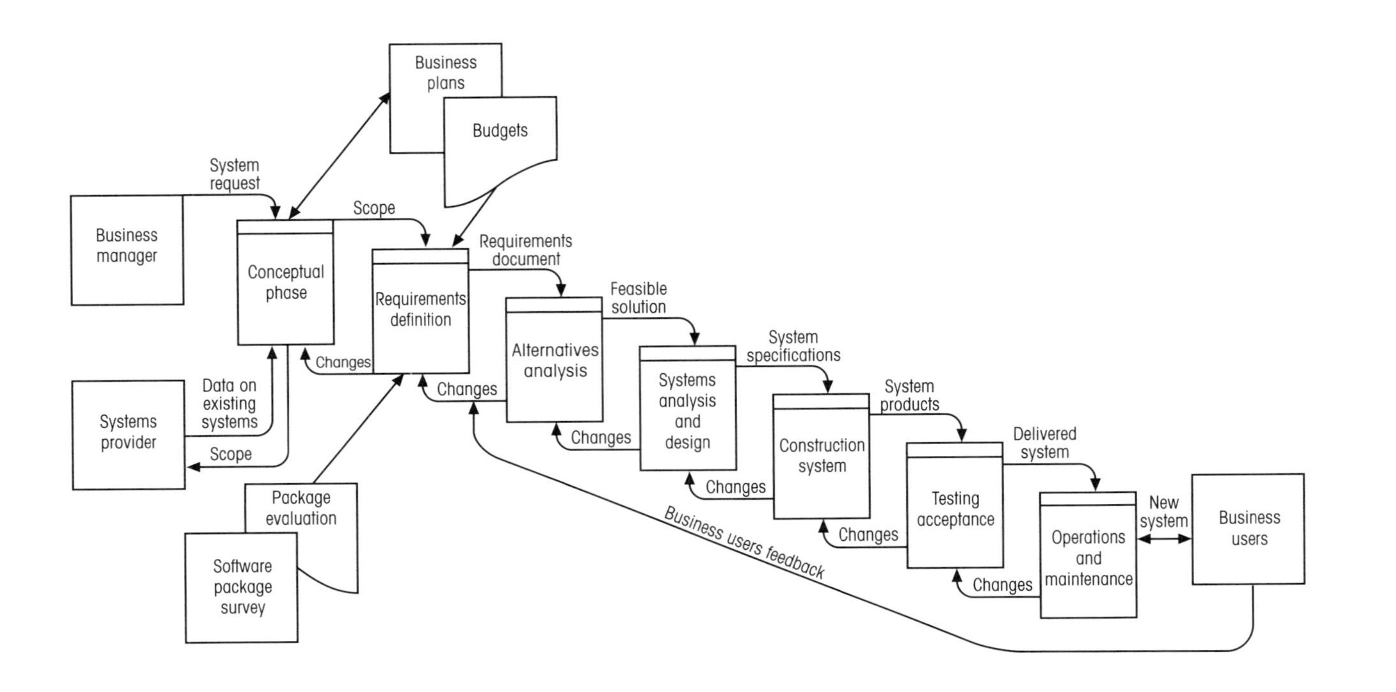

Figure 1.4. A generic system development process.

managers can rightfully expect from the information service provider; and, of equal importance, what the information service provider must receive in return if the IT application is to meet managerial expectations and add value to the business.

The technical language of the systems world is not used. Rather, a language that is by now familiar to most managers and information service providers is used. This is the neutral, but highly effective, language of quality management (QM).

By adding a dimension to the dialogue between business managers and information service providers, the language of QM eases the managers' problem in making system decisions. This is an improvement over the situation where managers are forced to make such decisions using only the language of the technology. The language of quality and the principles of QM are fully compatible with the process of systems development. Therefore, QM should be viewed by both business managers and information service providers as an opportunity to attain a high level of communication and understanding leading to improved performance and productivity in business systems. Hopefully, all parties using IT will develop a greater empathy for the problems of each other and come to understand that partnership is the key to successful uses of computer and communicating technologies.

The book proceeds as follows: Chapter 2 briefly discusses the requirements for IT support commonly required by business managers. How important are these requirements to the success of the business? How are business requirements for automation support best satisfied, and what are the respective roles of managers and information service providers in jointly accomplishing a successful implementation? The proper role of IT is presented, and reasons for the historic poor performance of IT systems are examined.

While the book assumes a general knowledge of the principles of quality management, chapter 3 presents a generic description of those principles. This will provide the language of quality for use in the remaining chapters.

Conditions influencing the computer industry are presented in chapter 4. These are examined to the extent that they increase the risks associated with an IT project. This discussion assesses the computer industry and marketplace, and identifies those conditions that make the successful use of IT difficult.

The remainder of the book examines the proper way to automate a business requirement by using a neutral example—building a custom home. The process of home construction closely parallels the systems development process and provides a nontechnical basis for discussing systems development expectations, issues, problems, strategies, roles, and responsibilities. Using this example is also key to the continuing QM evaluation, which must be performed by the business managers of the information systems provider. This evaluation is based on the premise that quality homes or quality and valued information systems cannot result from a construction process that does not promote quality. In other words, it is fairly easy to predict the final structural (not cosmetic) quality of a product by examining the quality-promoting activities of the process used in construction.

Structural quality is differentiated from cosmetic because the appearance of quality can be tacked onto a structurally unsound house or system for marketing and sales purposes. In housing construction, there are certain safeguards against such practices (for example, independent inspections). In the information technology industry there are few such safeguards, and most business managers know nothing of them. So knowledge and evaluation of the information service provider's work processes are critical to making an informed judgment about the likelihood of ending up with a quality system or service.

In conclusion, the book provides a summary guide of the major activities that should be observable during a soundly managed systems development effort. Finally, it can be used to determine the degree to which development activities have been documented. This last element, documentation, can prove critical in an attempt to bring or defend against legal action should system failures result in damage to a business or any of its customers.

CHAPTER 2

Requirements for Quality Information and Systems

Introduction

This chapter identifies the requirement for quality information and systems in support of business activities, and relates those requirements to what can be provided by IT. Note what is addressed: what IT can reasonably accomplish, not necessarily all that is advertised as possible. Determining the effective and cost-efficient use of these technologies is one of the most difficult decisions facing business managers. These decisions concerning what IT should do require considerable thought and must take several nontechnical, cultural, social, and organizational factors into account. In chapters 5–9, the process for accomplishing this analysis and an introduction of the players required to properly perform it are explored. What follows is a discussion as to why such deliberateness is necessary.

Computers Are Exacting

While it is agreed that computers are amazing machines, it must be emphasized that they are extremely demanding in their use. This means that in their application, the workplace environment in which they are used must be carefully considered to ensure that a *net positive* impact is realized. Further, this impact should result in an economic gain for the business or at least not the imposition of an economic burden. Some members of the business community have begun to question the economic case previously made for much of today's automation. There are those who want to know the payoff for past automation investments. There are those who are even beginning to question the assumption, previously accepted as an article of faith, that automation always results in productivity improvements. In his 1992 book, *Managing for the Future*, Peter Drucker expresses this concern as follows (p. 96).

> The investment in data-processing equipment now rivals that in materials-processing technology—that is in conventional machinery—with the great bulk of it in services. Yet office and clerical forces have grown at a much faster rate since the introduction of information technology than ever before. And there has been virtually no increase in the productivity of service work.

So what should nontechnical business managers expect for their automation dollar? In truth, the principle expectation should echo Hippocrates' age-old admonition to the physician, "First, do no harm!"

Any application of IT needs to be done with caution. Note again in Figure 1.2 that the success rates of automated systems in the workplace have been somewhat discouraging. A 20 percent success rate, in another line of work, might equate to 4 out of 5 hamburgers being thrown out at a restaurant or only 2 out of 10 automobiles passing final inspection. If 80 percent of IT efforts are considered marginal successes or failures, what is the inevitable impact on the business where such systems are operated? It would seem fair to assume that where business is still being conducted, it is being done at a cost that was never anticipated either by business managers or employees. From the managers' perspective, increased business efficiencies have come only after resource and time expenditures far exceeded even the most pessimistic estimates. From the employees' perspective, increased business efficiencies have generally come through the imposition of extra workloads and long hours. This increased worker burden is usually the result of having to expend unbudgeted time and effort in the unexpected care and feeding of the computer. This unexpected care comes out of the hide of employees and is often exacerbated by the fact that personnel cuts have already occurred, having been promised in the original cost/benefit argument for the system. Also, rarely do system estimates include proper training or technology transition time; and they never account for the human burden experienced should the system not live up to the promises of the marketing brochure. As Figures 1.1 and 1.3 depict, a misallocation of tasking can occur, and the organizational and social aspects of the work process may not be properly addressed in the system's design.

With this reality as background, what can business managers realistically expect from an IT initiative? Managers must expect, and work to bring about, the successful insertion of IT into the business' work processes. Technology must assist, not hinder or hamper, the delivery of quality products and services to the revenue-providing customers of the business. Since IT's promise has often been oversold, the discussion begins with how to set realistic expectations for the use of information processing techniques.

Information Is a Critical Business Resource

To formulate realistic expectations concerning the use of IT, an understanding of the role that information plays in the management of a business is needed. Traditional management instruction holds that managers have three resources that must be successfully orchestrated if a business' goals are to be achieved. These three resources are personnel, money or capital, and the materials used in the construction and delivery of a product or service. To economists, these are the factors of production. Regardless of business, it is easy to understand, confirm, and identify this concept within a company. What is not so obvious is the role and relationship that information plays in this concept. Essentially, information, and the data from which information is formulated, needs to be viewed as a fourth resource of management equally important as the other three. In fact, it can be argued, information is more important that the other three resources. How can this be possible?

The critical nature of information, and the technology used in its processing, lie in the fact that knowledge about the condition and status of the other resources comes to managers in the meanings that information can portray. Unless the business is small enough for all activities to be directly observable, management's understanding of what is going on is based on these information portrayals. Decisions concerning the company's future are largely based on the relevance and accuracy of the information presented to the decision maker. For example, the reality of inventory levels are not generally being observed, only the reality as perceived through an inventory report. Unless the business manager personally conducts a physical shelf inventory, reorder decisions are made on the basis of an inventory report either prepared by another person or calculated using data from some other process such as a point-of-sales system, with data collected by an electronic checkout system. These same reality through information dependencies exist with countless other applications from banking to hospital administration, from air traffic control to medical diagnoses and treatment.

The more direct human observation and involvement are reduced and replaced with information technology, the more precise must be the analysis, design, and development of the systems that gather, process, and deliver information to human decision makers or other automated decision points. To the degree that human experience and judgment are removed, the information must portray reality in absolutely clear and accurate terms that cannot be misunderstood or misinterpreted by a decision maker far removed from the action.

To the degree that such information, even under the best of circumstances, is open to misinterpretation and misunderstanding, human experience and judgment must remain in the process.

Characteristics of Quality Information and Systems

The critical relationship between information and the other resources available to management is such that the other resources cannot be effectively and efficiently managed unless information used in portraying their reality is accurate and timely. This allows management to make its required decisions or to take its related actions, such as planning future strategies or controlling current operations. For most businesses, the application of IT commonly includes the following:

- Reports to management
- Storage and retrieval of business records
- Order processing and billing
- Transaction processing
- Financial management
- Inventory management
- Personnel and payroll
- Word processing

It is easy to see the importance of quality information to each of these functions and, in turn, to the successful operation of the business. In most instances, information processed by the application represents the changing status of corporate resources central to the delivery of a product or service to a corporate customer. In all cases, the presence and use of poor quality information has a detrimental effect on the business' internal operations, the lives of employees, and customer relationships. But how can poor information be prevented? By defining, designing, constructing, and operating each application system in such a way that its outputs (that is, information) possess the attributes of quality and the degree of precision required to support the business activity. For most uses, quality information is thought to possess the following attributes. It is *accurate, timely, relevant,* and *confidential.*

To guarantee information quality, the quality of the manual and automated processes that capture, store, retrieve, manipulate, and deliver information must be improved. Quality information cannot come from poor quality processing systems. Like information, quality processing systems possess certain attributes. From the employees' perspective, a quality system is *accurate* and *correct; easy to use; consistent;* and *available* when needed.

From a systems administrator's perspective, a quality system should be easy to *maintain; adaptable* and *flexible;* well *documented;* and *reliable.* The corporate auditor views a quality system as one that is well *documented, auditable, verifiable, consistent,* and *secure.* Finally, corporate management views a quality system as one that has all of the listed attributes, plus one that is *effective* and *cost-efficient*.

Collectively, it is desired that the use of automation result in no adverse consequences due to the information being inaccurate, out of date, or irrelevant to its intended use. Further, it is necessary that business secrets and personal privacy not be compromised. Finally, the system must be auditable and cost-efficient.

This is a tall order for any IT system as the audit community has been pointing out for the last 20 years. Time and again auditors have demonstrated that automated systems deliver inaccurate information, lack internal controls, lack security and privacy controls, are open to fraud and abuse, and possess inadequate audit trails. During the same 20 years, managers and users have observed that IT systems are poorly documented, insufficiently tested, difficult to use, and are a runaway expense. Taken as a whole, these criticisms describe systems that are generally unreliable. Unreliable, and yet becoming more integrated into the day-to-day operation of businesses.

If supported by unreliable information processing systems, the quality of business service will always be less than desired. Unreliable means that the processing system and its information output cannot be trusted. No matter how much they are customer-focused, sensitized, motivated, or empowered, employees cannot consistently perform above the level of support they get from their IT systems. When computer output is inaccurate, it is wrong! (Users, however, may not know it.) When the system is unavailable, it is down! When they cannot sign on, employees cannot provide service to the customer! When the index pointers fail, the database has to be reconstructed. When software is not adequately tested, the system produces errors. When edit programs don't catch errors, the database gets corrupted! When the database is corrupted, damage of unknown dimensions can occur to the business. When systems documentation is not current, software problems cannot be corrected! These examples are more commonplace than acknowledged by most technologists. The adverse impact on business operation is more serious than most business owners will admit, even to themselves.

These examples can certainly begin to account for the 80 percent marginal failure rate noted in Figure 1.2. A reasonable analogy to the insertion of IT into a business organization is to implant a medical device into a living body. The range of outcomes is similar. If the medical procedure is successful, the person's health is enhanced. If the procedure is not successful, the body may reject the implant. If information technology insertion is not successful, a business may actually reject the information system as *foreign* and revert to its previous way of working. Such rejection is rarely simple; however, as a great deal of capital, prestige, and emotional investment has been made in the new system and considerable pain will probably be experienced before the rejection is actually allowed by management to become official.

Note that the business initially sought the IT implant because of business health reasons. After rejection, the original unhealthy conditions will still exist and the resources and lost time coupled with the stress of rejection may well prove terminal.

Continuing the analogy, another outcome could be that the medical implant functions, but complications set in that must be treated with massive doses of drugs. Such secondary problems have a direct corollary with an IT insertion and are exemplified by employee resistance, the creation of unsanctioned work around procedures, problems of worker health and stress, unanticipated trauma, and repairing damaged relations with customers and other inconvenienced parties.

Note that with this outcome, the business may actually experience more problems of a secondary nature than is justified by the originally perceived benefits of the IT system. This implies that the ripple effect of technological impacts on a business needs to be examined.

A final possible outcome in the implant analogy is death of the organism. This can result from too little, too late, or when the stress induced by attempting to accommodate to the technology ends in some catastrophic failure with the customer community, or through slow financial hemorrhaging as care and feeding expenses continue to grow with no offsetting increase in revenues realized.

The actual frequency of the outcomes reflected in Figure 1.2 are the estimates made by A. Mowshowitz of the impact on organizations of IT systems in North America. His research suggests that about 20 percent of systems achieve something of their intended benefits, 40 percent make a marginally positive impact on the organization, while the final 40 percent fail or are never completed (Eason 1988). While no comprehensive survey seems to exist for Great Britain, a limited number of studies indicate similar figures. Of 20 office automation efforts sponsored by the Department of Trade and Industry (DTI), only 15 continued past a trial period and many of these had not achieved the planned objectives (DTI 1986). Wroe (1986) examined 10 systems implemented by small construction companies. Four were considered a success, four were discontinued, and in the remaining two cases, the firms were still struggling after a long implementation period.

Consequences of Poor Quality Information and Systems

The estimates presented in Figure 1.2 warn of the potential for adverse operational impacts of IT on a business. This is certainly a reality that should not be experienced. Another related consequence looming over the use of automation by a business is the potential for legal liability. The ever-increasing dependence on automation is creating situations where system and software failures can result in significant business foul-ups, many of which have legal implications. For example, consider the following:

- The well-publicized delays involving the opening of the new Denver Airport have revolved around "errors in the software that control its automated baggage system. Scheduled for take-off by last Halloween ('93), the airport's grand opening was postponed" (Gibbs, 1994, 86). Losses at the rate of $1.1 million a day have been calculated. As of February 1995, the airport was scheduled to open by March 1, 1995, with a manual baggage system.

- Only six years ago, the information network at Westinghouse Electric was being celebrated as a marvel to behold. The Westinghouse System... was able to slash inventories by 25 percent, cutting billions of dollars out of the inventory investments.... Unfortunately, that exemplary system hasn't kept Westinghouse from having to take more than $4.1 billion in write-downs since then.... The financial services arena, which was the most heavily served...sank into the red. (Reprinted from *Financial World,* 1328 Broadway, New York, NY 10001. Copyrighted ©1994 by Financial World Partners. All rights reserved.)

- When a hospital bookkeeping system's software failed, at least 100 hospitals had to incur costs involved in switching to manual bookkeeping. While permanent data were not lost and no threat to patient treatment occurred, the installation of manual procedures posed additional operating costs ("Program errors halt hospital computer works," 1989).

- The Bank of America brought its new trust accounting and reporting system on-line before it was fully debugged in order to replace an aging system. The new system crashed for days at a time, resulting in costly delays in trading securities in pension and trust funds valued at more than $38 million for more than 800 corporations, unions, and government agencies (Zonana 1987).

- A Minneapolis public relations firm switched to a new accounting and billing system, hoping to save staff time by dismantling the old system before installing the new one. When the new system failed to work, customers could not be billed for months, and even then manual methods had to be used. This led to a substantial cash flow crunch, causing the firm to depend on interest-bearing loans until the situation was corrected (Neumann 1988).

A small company might well have been forced out of business by such failures. These examples illustrate business damages primarily resulting from erroneous information being used by the business activity. They also, however, clearly point out that information quality is only part of the equation. The integrity, dependability, and reliability of the information processing system constitutes the other parts. As software systems become more embedded with, and integral to, such critical functions as air traffic control, nuclear power plant control, and medical equipment operation, the chance for substantial damage and resultant litigation grows.

Also, increasing numbers of systems operate in real time, thereby decreasing or totally eliminating the safeguard of human intervention. In these cases, the processing logic, algorithms, procedures, and so on must be of the highest integrity. It is no longer a question of correct information being acted upon by the business manager. It has become a situation where the business manager is being replaced by software, hardware, memory devices, and communications equipment that attempts to execute human judgment and carry out actions. This is where expert systems and concepts of artificial intelligence are heading: the eventual replacement of the need for human intervention and judgment.

Examining Figure 1.1 again, the strengths and the reason to use automation is to accomplish certain tasks better than a human. These applicable uses are characterized by speed, high volumes, vast storage and retrieval requirements, high accuracy (that is, calculations), and a boring repetitiveness that results in human loss of concentration. These applicable uses are not characterized by a need to correlate differing elements of information into meaningful patterns based on knowledge or experience. These uses do not require the degree of judgment normally thought of as human. These uses do not generally communicate directly with customers except in carefully defined routine matters such as ATM machines. Computers are not able to resolve customer service problems. For example, think of the growing level of frustration experienced as customers are increasingly forced to deal with corporate and government automated telephone answering systems. No one argues their benefit to record messages, but with informational, customer order, or problem resolution tasks, they cannot measure up to a real live person on the line.

Unfortunately, there are more serious and frightening consequences of poor quality systems than mere frustration and inconvenience. In many of these cases, human involvement in the process has been totally usurped, with information generation, control, and use being given over to an automated processing system. Or, as is more often the case, the human element is merely overwhelmed by a poorly implemented system that, in a crisis, can realistically be controlled by no one!

- A software error involving the operation of a switch on the Therac-25, a computer-controlled radiation treatment machine, delivered excessive amounts of radiation, killing at least four people (King 1992).

- In 1980, a man undergoing microwave arthritis therapy was killed when the therapist reprogrammed his pacemaker. He subsequently died as a result of his trauma (Neumann 1985).

- On Saturday, August 6, 1988, Heathrow Airport was due to handle some 830 takeoffs and landings when the air traffic control system failed. In the first five months leading up to the airport failure, there were five similar software problems (Lamb 1988).
- Indeed, programming or design errors have resulted in the ozone hole over the South Pole remaining undetected for years. Surprising as it may seem, the programs actually rejected the ozone readings they were registering at the time because they were so low. They were regarded as spurious. In other words, deviations from the expected norms were so extreme that they were discounted and assumed to be errors (*New York Times* 1986).

Peter Neumann, editor of *Software Engineering Notes*, advised that "if something you really care about (such as lives, money, resources, just plain data, or even the survival of the world) is to be entrusted to a computer system, you should all be very suspicious." In fact, he suggested that when the real risks become too great, managers and workers had better rethink the use of computers in those applications (Neumann 1989).

Conclusion

If system and software failures are so commonplace and oftentimes disastrous, what can be done? Why cannot the potential for failure be eliminated? How can business managers cope with such a reality and reduce risk to the business activity? The next two chapters set the stage for making the improvements necessary to overcome the rather poor track record of the past. First, managers must be aware of the powerful principles of QM and how these can be used to improve any process, including the process whereby technology is applied to a business problem. Second, business managers need some understanding of the culture and prevailing dynamics of the IT industry so that wise choices can be made regarding the selection of IT provider, automation strategies, and the management of technology specialists required to implement such strategies.

CHAPTER 3

The Principles of Quality Management

Introduction

This chapter presents a working concept of QM that can be referred to again and again. These concepts originate from the work of well-known experts in the quality and performance management field. One particular set of guru principles is not proposed. I believe that a small application of any of them would result in significant quality improvements for the IT industry and the customers of IT systems and services.

As in my book *Information Service Excellence Through TQM,* the QM approach summarized here represents the proven, pragmatic, and successful principles advocated by Mike Crouch and the consultants of the LEADS Corporation of Greensboro, North Carolina. The consolidation of expert theories into practical guidance and principles belongs to LEADS.

Interpretation of these principles to the IT industry belongs to me, as I have applied them to technology companies and at the University of Maryland in a graduate-level course titled "Total Quality Management for the Information Services Organization." This chapter is certainly not meant to be an exhaustive treatment of QM. It is merely designed to equip business managers with enough knowledge of QM principles to construct a QM profile of prospective IT providers and suppliers, and to understand which principles should be practiced during the phases of development when IT is applied.

Definitions and Terms

QM is defined as a management process to instill a culture of continuous improvement in an organization. Such improvements balance productivity increases against established quality improvement goals.

The principles of QM that support a philosophy of continuous improvement can be categorized as follows:

1. Recognize the need to improve goods and services.
2. Meet requirements by focusing on customers.
3. Set error-free work as the goal for all activities.
4. Manage by prevention.
5. Identify and monitor the cost of quality.
6. Measure performance of the business processes.
7. Adopt a problem-solving and corrective action process.
8. Obtain and sustain top management commitment.

The philosophy of continuous improvement has two primary objectives.

1. Provide the tools, techniques, education, and management required for continuous quality and productivity improvement.
2. Allow employees to work as a team to achieve quality and productivity improvements.

Successful implementation of a QM program that ensures continuous improvement must focus on taking a technical as well as a behavioral journey. The technical journey addresses the specific disciplines and methodologies of the business activity. The behavioral journey addresses the organizational issues, human resource development concerns, and the management practices used for the technical activity.

To ensure success of the behavioral journey and the eventual effectiveness of the technical journey, organizations need to institutionalize the management of change. To do so is to deal with the organization's culture. To address such issues, cultural change committees need to be formed to handle issues relating to management, measurement, education, and employee involvement.

These committees, working separately and together, create the environment for success of the entire QM effort. Such committees are comprised of senior and mid-level managers responsible for the overall supervision of the business activity.

Since, according to Deming, 85 percent of quality problems lie within the realm of management control, it is imperative that these committees be formed and empowered to function as an extension of executive management.

By focusing the QM effort on continuous improvement, the following can be expected.

- Communications become more effective since feedback from customers and employees is encouraged.
- Relationships between customers and suppliers are improved.
- Problems are anticipated, and many are eliminated.
- Wasted time and effort are reduced, and productive time is increased.

Recognize the Need to Improve Goods and Services

In a general sense, recognizing the need to improve quality centers on trying to sensitize people to the fact that commonly expressed levels of performance, while seeming to be high, may be completely unacceptable when viewed from the customers' perspective. The following examples are often used to illustrate what 99.9 percent accuracy really means to customers (Crouch 1992).

- At least 20,000 wrong drug prescriptions each year
- More than 15,000 newborn babies dropped by doctors or nurses each year
- Unsafe drinking water almost one hour each month
- Two short or long landings at major airports each day

- Nearly 500 incorrect surgical operations per week
- 16,000 lost articles of mail per hour

It would be interesting to know how many of these examples have their origin in the poor application of IT systems.

Another reason for embracing QM is the need to be able to adapt to change. As shall be seen, QM provides an excellent forum not only to adapt to change, but also to anticipate change. This means the ability to respond to changing markets, technology, and competition, and the impact these changes may have on a company's social structure, revenues, and profitability. By using QM mechanisms to anticipate change, the opportunities presented can also be explored and potential problems identified and mitigated. Used in this way, QM becomes an integral part of corporate risk management and strategic planning programs.

Meet Requirements by Focusing on Customers

This principle of QM incorporates the concept of the customer. The objective is to *establish a common understanding of quality with the customer.* The critical nature of this understanding should be clear. Without it, satisfying the customers' expectations becomes a crapshoot.

Meeting customer requirements, then, must first concentrate on the commonly used definitions of quality. Given the product or service, how will customers judge quality?

There are five generally accepted working definitions of *quality.*

1. *Transcendent*—You *know* what it is, but it cannot be precisely defined. You *know* by comparison.
2. *Product-based*—Precise measurement of some attribute—the more of the attribute, the higher the quality.
3. *User-based*—Highly subjective, since quality is the degree to which a specific product satisfies the wants of a specific consumer.
4. *Manufacturing-based*—Quality means conformance to a measurable and documented requirement (a specification). Quality is the degree to which a product or service conforms to the specification.

5. *Value-based*—Quality is perceived and discussed in relation to price. How much excellence can you afford?

Agreeing on which definition prevails is the important first step. This agreement determines what the developer of the goods or service has to produce, and how the customer will judge the goods and services. For example,

- Customers know what quality is when they see it versus agreed-upon acceptance criteria. Unless money is no object, this is a losing situation for the developer.
- Higher quality versus higher cost. What can customers afford? What features are they willing to pay for?
- Customer wants versus customer needs. A classic problem for the IT provider—separating wants from needs. Needs are job-based while wants are subjective.
- Conformance to specification versus satisfying expectations of the customer.

Later chapters explore how critical this mutual agreement can become to an application of information technology, and the many ways it may be expressed and measured. Without agreement, an IT project is destined to fail.

Meeting customer requirements demands that business actions be framed in the familiar paradigm of the customer-provider-customer relationship. *Everyone is someone's provider, and everyone is someone's customer* (Crouch 1992). This new framework includes all people we come into contact with, both inside and outside the enterprise (Figure 3.1).

While meeting the requirements of the external customer pays the bills, sensitivity to the internal business customer determines the effectiveness and efficiency with which the external customer is satisfied. Given a clear understanding of the external customer's requirements, meeting them in an economically efficient manner is the work of dealing with the requirements of the internal customers.

In a general sense the term *customer* seems rather clear. But for the automated information services provider such is not the case. While the

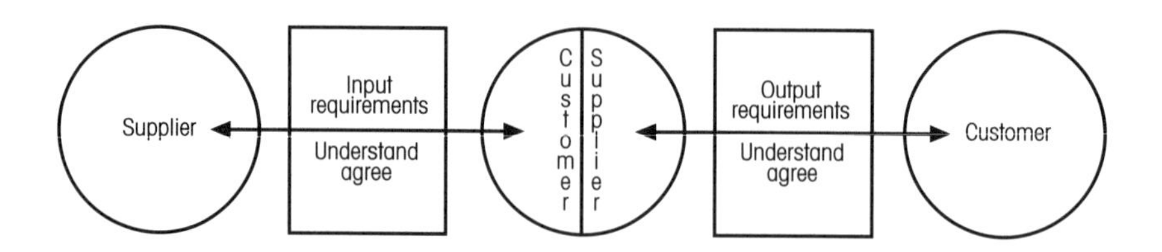

Source: Adapted from J. Michael Crouch, *An Ounce of Application Is Worth a Ton of Abstraction* (Greensboro, N.C.: LEADS Corporation, 1992): 6.

Figure 3.1. Each job (your job).

information services term for customer, *user*, seems straightforward, users actually represent many different customer interests that must be represented in the definition, design, and acceptance of an information system or service. This existence of multiple customers poses special problems when attempting to meet customer requirements. More on this later.

Set Error-Free Work as the Goal for All Activities

Do right things right the first time (Crouch 1992) (DRTRFT) is viewed by some as the mantra of QM. It sets the goal for a continuous improvement effort, and is the motivating reason for all QM activities.

At first glance DRTRFT seems to be an overly clever statement. It smacks of motherhood, the flag, and apple pie. It inevitably provokes derision and will be compared to zero defects, management by objectives, zero-based budgeting, quality circles, and other recent doctrines that have tried to revolutionize the way business is done. Blunting such knee-jerk criticism becomes an exercise in persuasion!

To properly define what DRTRFT really means, the following phrases and what they indicate must first be analyzed.

Do right things	= Reach agreement with customers on how quality is defined and measured.
	= Obtain requirements from all appropriate customers.

= Perform the requirements definition process correctly.

Right the first time = Work processes used to satisfy requirements are technically correct, efficient, and cost-effective.

= Work processes are efficient. They are working well with little waste.

= Work processes are effective. They are producing the desired results.

If DRTRFT is split into a requirements definition phase (DRT) and a systems construction and delivery phase (RFT), alternatives to DRTRFT can be postulated. For example,

Do Wrong Things Right the First Time (DWTRFT). Performing an analysis similar to the preceding one would indicate that with DWTRFT there is a problem with the requirements definition process and a failure to reach agreement on what quality means to the customer and how it will be measured.

It matters little that the product is efficiently constructed. It may even be considered a quality product. It does not meet the customer's requirements. It is the wrong product. For example, you order a double hamburger with cheese but get a chicken fillet. At the drive-thru, of course, no simple exchange is possible. No doubt it is a quality chicken fillet, but it is not what you ordered. Your impression of service quality goes down.

Do Right Things Wrong the First Time (DRTWFT). This version indicates difficulty in the construction and delivery of the product or service to specification. There is a clear requirements statement. The specifications include an understanding of how the quality of the product or service will be measured. Suppliers cannot just deliver. When and if they do deliver, the cost far exceeds their estimate because they had to do the job more than once. The classic example is probably the automobile recall. Detroit may indeed spend several years in designing and specifying the requirements of a new car, but flaws in the construction phase result in costly recalls and tarnishes customer opinion of the company.

Do Wrong Things Wrong the First Time (DWTWFT). This probably seems a joke to most people. After all, how often could you get the requirement wrong, the specifications for quality wrong, and the construction wrong? Maybe after reflection, DWFWFT explains the extremely low customer satisfaction indicated in Figure 1.2. What else but a bad case of DWFWFT could explain it?

What is error-free work and what constitutes an error-free mind-set? First, error-free work is not a motivation program; it is not a ploy to get everyone to work harder. Error-free work does not concentrate on the individual worker. Error-free work

- Recognizes that it is always cheaper to DRTRFT.
- Believes every error has causes that can be identified and eliminated.
- Organizes and plans every job with the goal of error-free work.
- Plans measurable improvement toward the goal of error-free work.
- Asks what went wrong, not who did it.

Without the right culture (acceptance of what is wrong without fixing blame), answers to the question, *what went wrong* cannot be obtained.

Manage by Prevention

The fourth principle of QM is managing by prevention. This is the process by which error-free work is planned and realized.

In Figure 3.2, the past/present curve illustrates the way things have historically been done. That is, with too little up-front planning and prevention, while letting the customer act as the final inspector.

Managing by prevention creates a future curve where time is allocated and spent practicing prevention. Thus, fewer efforts are needed to make things right after the customer receives the service or product. Managing by prevention also eliminates the primary cause of poor quality perceptions that customers develop about an organization.

One of the major challenges of managing by prevention is the cultural impact it will have on the typical organization. This principle of QM questions how projects are planned, how contract terms and agreements are negotiated, and how management and employees are rewarded.

If the management style is reactive, this is reflected in the way the project is managed. If corporate advanced planning is not the norm,

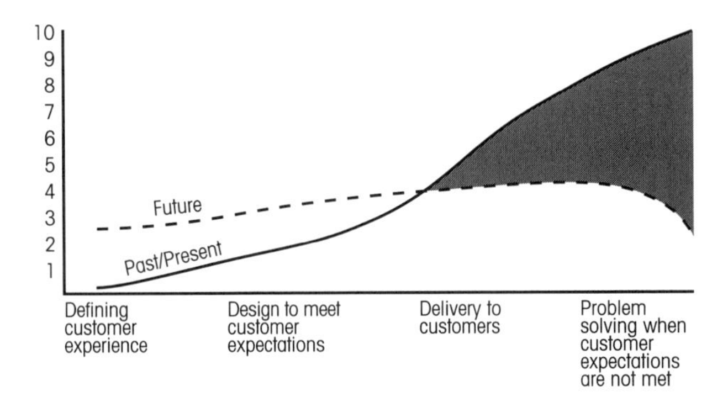

Source: Reprinted with permission from J. Michael Crouch, LEADS Corporation.

Figure 3.2. Effort by activity.

projects will follow suit. If project due dates are driven by unrealistic expectations, politics, or other factors, the time necessary to practice preventive management will undoubtedly be reduced. After all, the due date has already been set. Time cannot be wasted analyzing the project—just build it and deliver it. This, of course, perpetuates the reality of Figure 3.2.

Often, contractual arrangements do not encourage advance planning. For example, certain contracts allow the complexity and uncertainty of a task to be passed on to the customer, and reward little or no preventive thinking and poor planning. The cost estimates for such contracts are not going to be as well thought out as in the case where a product is expected for a fixed price. Such cost estimates often tend to be lowballed in order to get a foot in the door.

The issue of contract language also has a profound effect on planning. It is possible to have contract terms negate the preventive management philosophy of a QM effort. If it is assured, in contract language, that a supplier is able to pass complexity and uncertainty onto the customer, then there is little incentive to take a preventive management approach. It does not matter how well the supplier practices preventive thinking and advanced planning. It gets paid anyway because payment for the project occurs at various predetermined points. The practice of levying penalties for nonperformance may satisfy the contracting official, but it is of little practical use to the business manager who still has to get a job accomplished in spite of poor quality or late delivery.

In the final analysis, contracts that a company *lets* and contracts that it *obtains* should support, not contradict, the QM principle of preventive management that is fostered in the organization.

The last cultural aspect that preventive management brings into question deals with how and for what employees are rewarded. This raises the question of who gets rewarded—planners and preventive thinkers or firefighters. Remember, people do what they are rewarded for.

Do managers who practice error prevention, who plan a project with honest resource estimates, and who enforce standards get rewarded for such practices? Or do such attempts at rational management get slighted as the latest project in crisis gets resolved by the firefighters? The firefighters should have been practicing prevention all along.

As a result, does the reward and incentives system promote the mentality of catching problems at the end, regardless of cost? Notice that the main components of prevention are to anticipate, plan, and act. Firefighters, through inspection, tend to solve the same problems over and over again on project after project. In fact, it is sometimes wondered if such people create or purposely overlook problems so that they may assume the savior role later in the project's life.

Identify and Monitor the Cost of Quality

Cost of quality is critical for the long-term success of the effort. While it has been said by Crosby (1979) that quality is free, this can only be true in an environment where QM practices are already standard. Most organizations are not there yet, and so there will be certain ramp-up costs associated with institutionalizing QM principles and practices. Identifying and monitoring the cost to produce quality allows the initial expense of the ramp-up to be offset by actual benefits. Identifying and monitoring the cost to produce quality also allows organizations to specify the areas of the business process needing attention and improvement.

One way to express this thought is through another examination of Figure 3.2. The shaded area illustrates that the problem-solving activities necessary to meet customer expectations are a form of waste. Therefore, they represent lost resources and profit. This is a loss due to

- Right things done wrong.
- Wrong things done right.
- Wrong things done wrong.

These are *avoidable* costs of quality and they *need not* occur. It is common for such waste to represent more than 25 percent of revenues or budget. That is, a 25 percent improvement can be made in the financial picture of the enterprise by just eliminating such waste. In the private sector, this can be profits or investments for future competitiveness. In the government sector, a 25 percent improvement provides resources to meet new legislative mandates, cut into backlogs, or improve service to the public.

Quality does, however, require some expenditure of resources, but for preventive purposes! These are unavoidable costs if quality is to become a reality. While not reflecting all of the necessary expenditures, Figure 3.2 indicates these unavoidable costs are required for preventive thinking, advanced planning, and the design of error-free systems. This increase is illustrated by the raised future line over the past/present line. Other unavoidable costs of quality should include training and tools to better equip personnel to produce quality the first time.

Actually, resources are reallocated from the shaded or waste area to the front-end definition and design phases, where training, thinking, and planning prevent problems. These up-front increases in effort will result in sizeable reductions in the shaded or waste area, since the cost to solve and fix problems, after a product or service has been delivered to a customer, is much greater than preventing problems in the first place. Also, the impact of so-called intangible costs, such as loss of reputation, loss of credibility, and customer dissatisfaction, will be reduced. Organizations are spared the added costs and embarrassment associated with resolving problems once the product is in the customers' hands.

Finally, since product and service quality is a company's best advertisement, it is spared that portion of continuing expenses required to just hold onto market share. Since repeat business with satisfied, existing customers is more likely, the company can spend its marketing dollars to expand the business to new customers, rather than on repairing damaged relations with existing customers.

Measure Performance of the Business Processes

The objective of the sixth principle of QM is to gather and analyze data to support corrective actions and improvements to business processes. As a tool, measurement is vital if an organization is to know how its business is doing. Measurement of cost of quality, for example, helps to understand what it really costs to provide customers with a quality product or service. There is, however, great fear and trepidation at the thought of measuring anything that could reflect adversely on individuals, the group, or its management.

For this reason it is imperative that measurement activities not be perceived as the basis for adverse employee actions. Since candor in measurement—especially when reporting errors—is paramount, this point cannot be overemphasized. From experience it is clear that most employees perceive the use of measures as a front activity for layoffs and downsizing. Measurement programs are trusted only when they are believable. Remedial training and work process improvement efforts are perceived by employees to be the other side of the measurement game and equally important as tracking error rates and performance. One without the other won't be trusted. In the rare case (15 percent or less according to Deming), where an employee really appears to have made an error, close examination probably reveals problems with the training process, the supervision process, or the quality review process.

Once the process improvement and remedial training orientation of measurement is made evident to employees, real candor in reporting results. Truthfulness in measurement reveals the actual workings of business processes and serves as the basis for problem-solving and corrective action decisions.

What and how to measure should be determined by the affected work group; that is, what errors will be measured. Measurements must be objective; workers must be able to count occurrences of not meeting the requirement or the deviations from a standard. Measurements must be used positively to improve the work process, not to punish!

Finally, measurements are used to determine where an organization has been, where it is going, and how it is doing. Measurement allows management to take a snapshot of the business process at any point in time and monitor the pulse of customer satisfaction.

Adopt a Problem-Solving and Corrective Action Process

The purpose of this seventh QM principle is to institutionalize problem solving such that corrective actions actually solve problems more than once. The purpose, through analysis, is to get to the root cause of problems, and implement corrective actions aimed at that root cause, not just its symptoms.

Too often, problem solving has been viewed as those corrective actions taken to get a troubled product out the door! This type of activity is rework, not problem solving, and is a major contributor to waste.

Traditionally, problem solving does not occur until some crisis is encountered and management cannot tolerate the pain any longer. Then, hurriedly, some corrective action—aimed not at the problem but at the symptoms—is taken. Then it is back to work until the next crisis occurs. Nothing has changed. The work process and conditions that created the problem have not been addressed, so the same or similar problems are likely to recur. Furthermore, since the underlying causes have not been uncovered and analyzed, no early warning systems to keep management informed of developing future problems are devised.

Another major benefit of a problem-solving process is the ability to identify, through impact analysis, the ripple effect that even a seemingly minor problem can have on other work components. This impact, when cost of quality is calculated at each organizational point where the impact is felt, can be much larger than originally thought. The domino effect of quality problems in one work process affects the customer of that work process output, and the next and the next, as each subsequent customer has to undertake corrective cleanup work to make the work product usable. This can be especially insidious where information systems are concerned, because a lack of information quality is not readily apparent. Much is accepted as fact simply because the computer says so!

But how can problems in a work process be identified short of a crisis or a complaining customer? In a preventive vein, the people within the process can ask, what keeps me from doing my job right the first time? For example, such queries may establish that proper tools are not available; that standard work procedures are needed—or need to be enforced; that low quality supplies are inputs to the work process; and that more or better training is required. While some of these problems can be handled by the local supervisor, many will be beyond local management's control. Problems that involve other departments become increasingly difficult to address. Such problems require visibility and management commitment to solve. Interpersonal communications present the major hurdle. Use of a formal problem-solving process will gain everyone's attention and cooperation.

Such a problem-solving process, properly conducted, can answer the following questions.

- What is the problem? Be sure it is not people-oriented and that no finger-pointing is done.
- Where is the problem found?
- When did it happen?
- How big is it? What is the ripple effect or impact on subsequent customers? What is it costing?
- Is it growing?
- How will the organization know when it is solved?

The last question forces the identification of measures and the early warning indicators necessary to monitor for problem recurrence.

The most common group technique used for problem solving is brainstorming. It takes a product, service, or process that appears to be having problems and asks why. Phrased another way, with any satisfactory product, service, or process, ask, What could be done that would result in lowered quality and/or productivity?

Brainstorming assists teams in identifying elements of the problem or project. Group dynamics builds teamwork. Members of the team will have increased feelings of control over the job. This builds ownership of derived solutions and their implementation.

Since solutions may require the expenditures of resources, it is necessary to identify all current categories of waste and calculate a reasonable cost of quality related to the problem. This includes any ripple effect impacting other internal customers or external business customers.

In most problem-solving implementations the team performs a roadblock identification. Then it attempts to mitigate such roadblocks in the plan for corrective action implementation.

Obtain and Sustain Top Management Commitment

Was there ever an organizational improvement initiative that did not claim to require management support to be successful? On the other hand, when such initiatives fail, it is said that they lacked management support. This is true of QM, but there are several reasons why it should be easy to obtain and sustain management support for QM.

First, QM is not a separate activity laminated onto existing management practices. QM simply provides a focus of continuous improvement and prevention to the existing management process.

Both of these concepts support the goal of DRTRFT, which in turn results in satisfied customers and efficient use of resources. *What management would not support these objectives?* Furthermore, QM provides top management with a new perspective through which all organizational activity and initiatives can be viewed. Simply put, any business activity, current or planned, should be able to show a positive relationship to the following three questions.

1. What will the activity do to improve the quality of products or services?
2. If the activity is not helping customers reach their quality goals, why is it done?

3. If the activity is not helping to reduce avoidable costs of quality, why is it done?

Consistent use of these three questions can go farther to indicate management's commitment to quality than almost any other action. It forces all organizational elements to focus and articulate the quality relationship of all its activities, plans, acquisitions, and so on. It actually forces a sort of corporate quality impact analysis.

In addition to these three questions, top management commitment is demonstrated by the actions management takes to change the organizational culture and create an environment within which the practices of QM can flourish. These actions constitute the behavioral journey without which the technical journey cannot succeed.

Institutionalizing the Management of Change

To ensure success of the behavior journey and the eventual effectiveness of the technical journey, organizations need to institutionalize the management of change; that is, to deal with the organization's culture. The purpose of cultural change committees is to create an environment for success and to convey continuing top management commitment, support, and interest. There should be committees to address at least four major areas.

- Management
- Measurement
- Education
- Employee involvement

These committees should be staffed by senior and mid-level managers, perhaps even those most resistant to change. Each committee performs the following functions and reports to top management (that is, a steering committee).

- *Management committee*—This committee seeks out actions, which employees want to see and hear, that support the quality improvement process and makes sure there is a flow of these actions. The committee is empowered to make sure that all quality-oriented communications are clearly conveyed to all employees. It is responsible for scheduling and organizing appropriate events to reinforce participation and teamwork.

- *Measurement committee*—This committee determines areas, especially at senior levels of the enterprise, for measurement. These areas include high-level indicators dealing with external customers and their degree of satisfaction with the enterprise. Customer surveys are frequently used to measure such satisfaction. Internal measurement of work processes must be influenced by the measurements this committee determines are important to external customers.
- *Education committee*—This committee is responsible for arranging QM education to ensure knowledgeable employee implementation of quality practices, such as problem prevention and problem solving. This committee may also assume responsibility for ensuring that training in core business knowledge and skills is available and consistent with the organization's business and technical direction.
- *Employee involvement committee*—This committee is responsible for defining how the problem-solving and process improvement mechanism work. It designs a tailored procedure for the organization. The committee is also responsible for defining and implementing an employee/team recognition program that rewards prevention as opposed to firefighting.

Summary

This chapter has endeavored to impart a brief working knowledge of the generic principles of QM. This material is based on the extensive experience of the quality management consultants of the LEADS Corporation. In the remainder of the book, it will be shown how nontechnical business managers can use this familiarization with QM principles to meaningfully participate with their information services providers and to assist in determining whether or not the information services providers are following sound quality practices.

CHAPTER 4

Prevailing Conditions in the Information Technology Industry

Introduction

This chapter identifies characteristics and conditions of the IT industry that directly and importantly influence business managers' options and decisions. These characteristics and conditions are not widely recognized outside the industry, and yet their influence on attempts to successfully implement automation cannot be denied. For this reason, business managers must be aware of them and take them into account when planning IT initiatives.

Technology for the Sake of Technology

An overarching motivational factor for IT professionals is the economic need to continuously advance the technology and to personally stay current with the latest and greatest of those advancements. This is a technology where never-ending breakthroughs in speed, size, and economies of scale have resulted in an increasingly frantic pace in the race to market. It is an industry where the window of opportunity for the new is short, but the rewards are great for the few who capitalize on that window.

This is an industry where yesterday's proven solutions are not generally promoted because that technology is deemed outdated, and the challenge is to sell and master the new. It is an industry that has become self-perpetuating with each advance in technology, generating the need for new software and systems to utilize that technology, and new publications and training seminars to explain and sell the technology. With fundamental breakthroughs occurring at 18–24-month intervals, or as quickly as marketing departments can think up new buzzwords to describe existing technologies, users rarely see an actual working implementation of the last technological marvel before they are encouraged to embrace the next round of change. In truth, most technologies and their envisioned application never have the time to measure up to their marketed promise before something new is developed. The steady drumbeat is to always buy the newest. Nontechnical users are never told that software does not wear out—as do automobiles. Vendors just stop supporting the old and force users into the new. This form of obsolescence is very well planned, but it has little to do with the operational life of an integrated circuit or coded program.

From a career perspective, many in the industry view their greatest challenge as finding customers that will allow them to use the most recent technology—both hardware and software. To a certain extent this reality is understandable, but it must be consciously tempered with a strong sense of obligation to deliver, to those same customers, solutions that actually work using proven techniques and reliable software and hardware. This means that the preferred solutions to business processing problems or opportunities should probably be configured from components that have been well tested in the arena of the day-to-day workplace. The latest technological marvels being touted in contemporary industry journal advertisements generally do not exist except in carefully controlled settings. Most recent product announcements are still a long way from operating reliably in the workplace, with your employees as they attempt to satisfy your customers.

The cutting edge of technology may be a fine place for research laboratories and universities; but it can quickly become the bleeding edge for you with your business, career, and livelihood at stake. This is why it is so important that the initial consultive assistance you obtain be objective in orientation and driven to practical solutions.

In trying to be solution-driven, there is a fine line between using safe, traditional information processing approaches and pushing the envelope of technological application too fast in the name of a so-called strategic opportunity. Be too conservative and opportunities may be missed; be too aggressive and the project becomes too risky. Figure 4.1 depicts three critical relationships between a business, the influences of technology on a business, and the actual implementation of technology as subordinate to the business' objectives. These three boxes must be carefully balanced to get the greatest value from the use of technology.

The IT system (Box B) built for a business must be subordinate to the way a work process activity (Box A) is executed. (Box A represents the right side segment of process elements found in Figure 1.3.) Technological capabilities (Box C) are constantly changing, and some of these may profoundly affect the future ways in which a business process is conducted. Allowances for technological capability should be made when analyzing

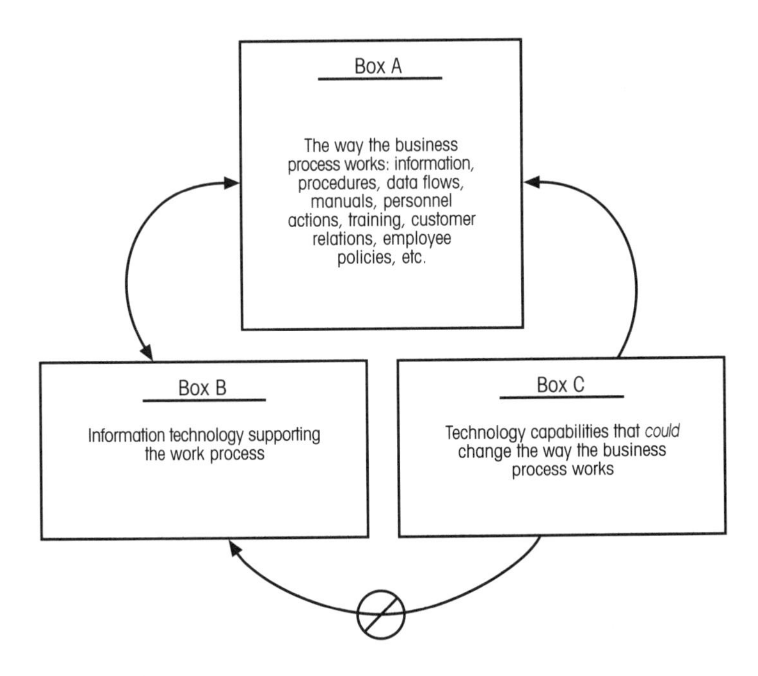

Figure 4.1. Relationships between a business, technology, and its implementation.

the way the current work process is executed. In other words, a solution-driven analysis of how technology could be used should always take into account Box C. If a new and proven technology can basically change the way a work process is executed, then that is all well and good. The work process (Box A) can be redesigned with appropriate changes made to the nontechnical work elements, as needed, while subordinate technical specifications are determined in light of overall changes to Box A.

This sequence of analysis allows new technology to be examined but always within the context of acceptable risk to the business activity being supported.

What must *not* be allowed to happen is a situation where the technological capabilities of the industry (Box C) directly influence the IT system (Box B) without first analyzing the potential impacts of the new technology on the business process (Box A). When this happens, automation no longer stays in its properly subordinate supporting role: It becomes the driver. As such, the technical portions of a business system may not smoothly integrate into existing procedures, workforce capabilities, and customer interface situations. Of course, the whole purpose of automation is to change the way business is conducted, but in positive ways. When technology becomes the driver, unforeseen negative impacts may be experienced. These must then be addressed through unplanned business process modifications, during which time the business and its employees and customers can suffer adverse side effects. These modifications also result in unplanned and unexpected expenses. Adherence to the perspective that Box C can influence Box B only after a Box A analysis helps ensure the rational use of technology. It also means that the likelihood of successful implementation is raised, and the business' risk is reduced. Investments will more likely result in desired improvements without being disruptive since IT has been kept in its appropriate supportive role.

The Crisis in Software Development

In chapter 2, some consequences of poor quality systems and software were discussed. Academic research into software engineering technologies is improving development methods and providing automated support tools. For example, prototyping and the use of formal validation and verification methods can minimize the introduction of errors and omissions when requirements are defined. Modular designs are used to contain processing functions so that inputs to and outputs from modules can be edited and controlled. Structured programming can minimize programming errors. Improved and even automated testing tools and techniques are now available, and with the advent of graphic modeling tools and desktop publishing, the ability to produce efficient and usable documentation has improved dramatically.

But, structured analysis, modular designs, thorough testing, and other development improvements for constructing and delivering reliable software and systems are perceived to add time and money to the programming of a new system. Reliability characteristics are seen to conflict with the need to introduce new software quickly. As organizations become increasingly aware of the possibilities provided by IT and the advantages gained from using software to perform critical functions, the demand for new software systems that are needed increases.

Studies have shown that the demand for new software is increasing faster than the ability to develop it. Moreover, the supply of skilled programmers is decreasing even as demand continues to grow. For the last decade enrollment in university computer science curricula fell as a percent of U.S. student population. Half of computer science students are foreign nationals, most of whom intend to return home upon graduation. Recent survey data reveal that interest in IT careers, after climbing to a level of 8.8 percent in 1982, is steadily declining and dropped to the level of 2.7 percent in 1989 (Rosenthal and Jategaonkar 1995). The vast majority of people who entered the profession in the mid-1960s with the advent of the IBM System/360 are going to retire by the end of this century.

Meanwhile, the rate of software growth is considerably greater than that of the economy. This ever-increasing software backlog provides a strong impetus for the early release of new software. Since testing typically comes toward the end of the development process and is usually the most difficult part of the programming effort to estimate, the need to meet deadlines forces the release of improperly tested systems. Moreover, it is felt that competitive advantage can sometimes be obtained by early release of software. This creates a situation that produces a great deal of bad software. Furthermore, the general buying public has come to accept, as normal, software that does not work properly. Software with bugs is sold before it is ready, and customers become the vendors' unwitting testers. When problems are experienced, customers who thought they were purchasing a finished product, often have to pay again for assistance sometimes through a 900-number setup. This may have become acceptable at the giant corporation or university, but it is an affront to managers of mid- to small-sized businesses who have already paid for what was thought to be a solution to a problem—not another problem requiring further expense.

Lack of Compliance to Standards

In this context, standards refer to those attempts by the IT industry to pronounce, for the *good of all*, an open measure of capability to which all suppliers will adhere. The good of all criterion has usually dealt with standards to ease the potential adverse impact on a business when selecting technical solutions by ensuring that several suppliers can meet the standard. The open aspect of this approach creates a competitive marketplace for buyers, eases transitions from one supplier to another, and provides an assurance that today's investment in technology will not be unnecessarily lost should users need to upgrade to increased capacity equipment.

Open standards are customer- and commerce-focused, and are promoted by suppliers when it is in their best interest. While vocally supporting open standards, most suppliers would much rather have the real world marketplace clamor for their proprietary ways of accomplishing information processing. From a marketing perspective, unless customers express an interest in, or demand, an open systems solution, suppliers will propose their proprietary approach.

This is certainly understandable from the suppliers' viewpoint. If I can lock you into my proprietary way of accomplishing your information processing requirement, chances are good that you will be my customer far longer than if I put you into the open systems world. This is especially true if my basic levels of quality and service leave you dissatisfied. In such cases, suppliers want your sunk costs, not their quality of service, to determine your future technology decisions. Also in such cases, quality of service may even deteriorate over time since you have been placed in a dependent position with no place to go without incurring great expense and inconvenience. A lack of adherence to standards can also be a major impediment to any attempt to expand IT to other functions within your business. On the other hand, an adherence to standards can make such expansions reasonably easy and cost-effective.

High Expectations—Overpromise, Underdeliver!

These descriptors of the IT industry are not meant to imply a deliberate pattern of business practice. To be sure, there have been instances when these conditions have been consciously exploited to clear inventories and make sales. But that is not the general rule.

Much more likely is a situation where unbridled enthusiasm for a particular technology or vendor, on the part of technologists, leads to the making of rosy predictions based on product assumptions and hoped-for unlimited funding by customers to make the promises a reality. The previously mentioned desire, on the part of technologists, to work with the latest and greatest is supported here by an optimism that all new technology can be mastered—given enough time and money. And it probably can, but at what cost to a business?

The vast majority of technology marketing tends to greatly oversimplify the complexities of using IT and underemphasize the need for careful analysis and planning of its implementation. By design, nontechnical people are usually left with the impression that the successful use of IT is almost as easy as pointing out the wall plug to the system installer. Additionally, this impression often includes the subtle hint that answering questions is beneath the technologists' dignity and that all will be well if users have faith and unlimited patience, and if they keep the money coming. The unhappy reality is that many technologists actually believe the marketing materials that are provided and do no critical assessments of their own before attempting an implementation in a business environment.

Shortage of Objective Analysts

As noted, there is an increasing shortage of the type of skilled systems analysts needed to initially assist business managers in determining the appropriate and beneficial use of IT. While many in the industry carry the title of systems analyst, it has no standard meaning, making the selection of an appropriate analyst for a given situation tricky.

Persons formally educated as systems analysts have been trained to examine component parts of a business system for interrelationships, problems, areas of improvement, solutions, and potential opportunities for competitive advantage. Analysts are tasked to disassemble systems into their component elements, examine the quality of work products passing between elements, identify deficiencies, and propose ways to improve the work processes of the overall business system. They then reassemble the components for increased efficiencies and effectiveness using IT where appropriate.

Formally educated systems analysts also disassemble business systems to examine the sources of information, how it is used, and the way it flows throughout the organization in support of business activities. This examination documents information processes from data origin to final archiving and attempts to identify where information is becoming distorted (causes) and how to improve the information's value (corrective actions or added processing). Such analysis requires a thorough dedication to the priorities of a business over technology and to people over machines. Such analysts treat hardware and software as tools that can enhance information usage but must never be allowed to dictate that usage. This type of analyst functions as a general practitioner does in the medical profession, dealing with the whole system, identifying symptoms, performing a diagnosis, and calling in specialists as needed. This type of analyst will present an array of information processing proposals, including cost and time estimates. These proposals will vary from slight, low-risk modifications of the current system to suggestions that entire processes be redesigned. This is not just reengineering hype; systems analysts have been redesigning business processes for over 30 years. Typically, this type of system analyst transfers the chosen systems design to other technical professionals who actually develop and deliver the final system. They often stay on to oversee the construction of the system, thus protecting the business managers' interests.

In chapter 5, this type of systems analyst is compared to the architect on a construction project. His or her first concern is for requirements and design, not the material means used in construction.

Others in the IT industry who carry the title of systems analyst include those who have become specialized in any number of technical support areas. These include the following:

- Database techniques
- Programming languages
- Commercial software packages
- Communication systems
  —Local area networks
  —Wide area networks
  —Data, voice, video, E-mail
- Equipment
- Image processing
- Security systems

To be specialized and truly expert usually means competence is limited to two or three languages, three or four software packages, or one or two vendor equipment lines.

It is entirely proper to refer to these individuals as systems analysts, since they are experts in the specifics of a particular support area of IT, and since they contribute to overall IT success by ensuring the optimal application of their specialties. But for the same reason, they cannot generally function as the overall information and architectural analyst. There is only so much an individual can master. While specialists are indeed experts in their respective areas, they do not generally possess the comprehensive experience to function in the high-level business/information requirements arena. Analysts that can operate at this level understand first how business and/or government operate. For them the up-to-the-minute specifics of technology come second. They understand that building a successful IT system is often more dependent on politics than on technology. They understand the need for sound project administration and customer expectations management. They have been responsible for system development efforts and their operation. They have been on the firing line. They have had successes and failures. They tend to be conservative regarding the degree of risk to which they will subject a client. They understand the principles of quality management and tend to show visible distress when they see them violated. They are willing to fight for what they believe is in the client's best interest. They are rare!

Competence and Viability of Suppliers/Providers

As would follow from the just-described conditions, another major characteristic of this young IT industry, which raises the risk factor of any automation effort, is the problem of incompetent or unviable suppliers. For viability, users must examine those business practices that evidence a commitment to the long-term reliability of system products and the economic stability of the supplier's enterprise. The exacting nature of computing and the discipline required to develop or tailor software to a specific business need demands a level of dedication and continuity of effort not required in most contract support arrangements. First, the seriousness of the relationship with the information systems provider is greater than with most other contractors. This seriousness is related to the fact that businesses are becoming increasingly dependent on the reliable, accurate, and uninterrupted operation of IT systems in their day-to-day activities. Second, support arrangements for IT systems tend to cost more in both time and money for a successful implementation than almost any other business undertaking. If the IT project has any significant impact on day-to-day business activity and is to be used by any number of employees, continuity of the supplier's workforce assigned to the project during development and installation is critical!

Finally, the nature and rate of change in the IT industry, coupled with its own evolving business requirements, mean that few IT projects are ever really completed. No matter how well the initial effort was planned, system upgrades, expansions, and occasional software and hardware maintenance are required as a business grows. All of this means that unless a business intends to assume maintenance and operational responsibility on an in-house basis, it will find itself in a long-term relationship with its IT provider.

So, how viable is the world of computer, software, and system providers? How can potential suppliers be screened to determine which ones are likely to be around five, three, or even one year from now? A recent count of the metropolitan Washington, D.C., area Yellow Pages identified over 100 pages of computer and related service suppliers. Other metropolitan areas have equally large populations from which to choose. The 100 pages were broken down into four general categories: computers–dealers; computers–software and services; computers–designers and consultants; and computers–training. For purposes of discussion, computer–dealers is disregarded until equipment decisions are made. Remember that the initial need is to define and describe, in technology terms, a business processing requirement. After agreement is reached on the requirement, discussion can begin on how to best satisfy needed technical capabilities using commercially available components. So it is premature to be working with computer–dealers, unless pre-existing hardware investments dictate a certain make and model for a project.

Remember also that the business activity to be automated will be performed by a combination of employees, procedures, software, and hardware components. To decide too early on hardware is to unnecessarily constrain the design of the processing system for a business.

The place to begin is with the systems designer/consultant community or the software services community. These were tallied at over 1100 listed sources just in the suburban Maryland Yellow Pages. These sources ranged from nationally known accounting firms and large computer service companies to individual consultants. It is a rule of thumb that of new businesses, the majority will not be around two years from now. So, identifying a competent and viable source of assistance is a task requiring careful research. Without the knowledge to objectively evaluate suppliers (this knowledge is what you are seeking), what can business managers do to raise the chances of selecting a competent and stable source of advice and consultation?

There are several courses of action. First, your state's Small Business Administration may have programs and educational materials to assist in identifying reliable consultation sources. There may also be training and education sponsored by the state. Second, the local community college or state university may be able to aid in selecting a competent and stable source of consultation. Third, many metropolitan areas have associations of retired business executives who work part-time in consultive capacities. These associations represent great pools of business experience that may be able to provide assistance. Individual consultants often belong to associations for educational and networking purposes. This is generally a desirable qualifier since it indicates a desire, on the consultant's part, to remain current and to have access to skills and knowledge not personally possessed. Some of these associations require members to subscribe to a code of behavior and ethics that strives to protect clients from common abuses found elsewhere in the industry.

Regardless of where information is sought, the business manager's inquiry needs to be carefully formulated to convey the following points.

- Assistance in determining the appropriate use of information technology for a business is requested.
- The objective advice of an experienced systems analyst who understands the limitations as well as the capabilities of computers, is sought.
- Assistance from someone who is connected to no particular hardware or software vendor is sought.
- Consultation from individuals who have actually implemented and operated an IT system in a workplace environment is sought. This is someone who has been responsible rather than someone who merely knows.

Beyond this initial screening, the routine business practices of checking with the Better Business Bureau, requesting a Dun and Bradstreet report on the company, and requesting references should be followed. The business practice of advertising for competitive bids also plays a part in obtaining competent suppliers, but this usually comes later in the project when actual hardware and perhaps software elements of the designed system are acquired. Competitive bids are only meaningful after a specification for hardware and software needs has been determined, and the business is seeking the best economic deal. Later chapters discuss this further. For now, however, a business is striving to obtain the expertise needed to formulate the specification statement that providers and suppliers will use in arriving at their work proposals and cost estimates.

Summary

The IT industry is a rapidly changing, highly competitive, unevenly staffed, and volatile arena within which business managers must seek answers to real and perceived information processing and technology questions. Depending on the extent of previous involvement with computers, these questions can run the gamut from an initial exploratory inquiry to interrogations regarding the best way to expand IT to other functions of the business. These questions can generally be summarized as follows:

- Can IT help a business become more efficient and effective? Can it help improve the bottom line? Can IT provide a competitive edge? Is there more potential payback from the automation investment than just that realized by reducing payroll?
- Is the current use of IT helping or hindering the success of a business? At what cost?
- Do you feel that you are getting value for your current IT dollar? Do you have any idea what your return on investment is?
- What is the quality of support from your IT provider?
- Is there a vague feeling that your business could be vulnerable to system interruptions, loss of data, or loss of key technology personnel?
- Are intelligible answers to your questions given by your IT provider?

The remainder of this book describes, through the use of an analogy, an environment in which a successful automated system can be developed. It stresses analysis, quality planning, and testing, and requires the proactive involvement of business managers with information technology specialists. It outlines an approach for assuring value for your technology dollars.

CHAPTER 5

Automating the Business Requirement (Part 1): Requirements Definition Phase

Introduction

Many automation projects suffer from communication problems that arise between nontechnical business managers and IT providers. It is rare that all parties to a business automation effort begin a project together and proceed in partnership from concept development through to implementation. More likely, business managers and their functional users, as well as IT managers and their analysts, move in and out of projects that are in the middle of some portion of multiphased development. Thus, difficulty of communications is due, in part, to people moving in and out of a project, trying to discern what has gone on prior to their arrival, what is expected at the moment, and what activities are still to come.

As is often the case, parties to the IT effort are not even in agreement as to the development steps to be followed in constructing a system that satisfies business requirements. Without this fundamental understanding and agreement, it is extremely difficult for project continuity to be maintained. If continuity does not exist, then a great deal of time and money is expended in continuously relearning where the project has been so that participants can figure out where to go. Since the business managers' primary objective is to satisfy a business requirement as quickly and cost-effectively as possible, it is clear that knowledge of and agreement with the project's steps and procedures used to meet the requirement are vital.

The concept of a systems development process is well understood by thoroughly educated systems analysts, since it has been taught for over 30 years in most IT degree programs. Referring, again, to Figure 1.4, the SDP is a systematic and analytic process where

- Development efforts are managed.
- Requirements are analyzed, defined, and specified.
- Solutions are explored and designed.
- Programs are coded; databases are built; and equipment and networks are procured.
- System components are arranged and tested.
- Systems are accepted for customer use.

Not all IT providers understand the importance of the SDP. In their desire to reduce expenses and maximize profit, not all IT providers apply the SDP as vigorously and conscientiously as high quality would demand.

Further, there are many in the IT provider community who have not been exposed to the SDP discipline. Because of their expertise in the use of specific off-the-shelf packages, the providers need only to be proficient with the package, not with the analysis steps and process that determine the why, where, or how of package use.

Additionally, some IT providers are inexorably linked to certain hardware, software products, and the product's approach for addressing a business problem. To them, every business problem looks the same and requires the same solution. Aside from the issue of questionable objectivity, such IT providers may have never been involved in an SDP analysis, except to convince a customer to buy some predetermined solution. It is important to be aware that many IT providers have never been involved in a cradle to grave development effort of any degree of complexity. Therefore, they only know bits and pieces of the entire process. Since this is the case, it is important for business managers to become familiar with the disciplined analysis imposed by the SDP. Since there is this wide variance of SDP understanding, and since the SDP is not universally accepted and applied by IT providers, nontechnical managers must become generally familiar with the process in order to protect their interests. It is much more advantageous for business managers to concentrate on the activity of the analytic thought needed to devise the correct solution to the business problem than it is to try—however valiantly—to stay abreast of a rapidly changing technology and attempt to make the correct hardware, software, and service decisions. The analytic work outputs and conclusions from a properly executed SDP will answer the hardware, software, and service questions, and will be based on analysis of the problem, *not* on glossy marketing materials and promises.

In this chapter, the degree of SDP knowledge needed by business managers is examined. Since the SDP itself has evolved into many expressions that are confusing even to IT practitioners, a nontechnical model of familiar complexity is presented as a neutral example against which business managers can evaluate development progress and formulate questions for project monitoring. The purpose is not to make systems development experts out of managers, but to better equip such managers to constructively converse with professional information technologists.

While business managers cannot expect to keep up with the jargon-laced solutions of the technologists, the managers can participate at the level of the analytic process being used to reach the technical solution. If rational analytic process steps have been ignored, circumvented, or are being used in defiance of common sense, business managers will know enough to view the project with a skeptical eye and begin to question the appropriateness of the project's direction even if not totally understood at a technical level.

Good, sound, and feasible solutions to complex business process problems and added-value opportunities do not result from ill-conceived project plans and poorly executed analytic processes. Feasible solutions for a successful implementation result from sound analytic work and competent management of the systems development and systems delivery process. Therefore, the health of any IT project can be surmised by examining and evaluating the process being used to define, design, develop, and deliver the information system or service.

But, without becoming systems analysts, how can business managers perform this type of examination and evaluation? What nontechnical model could be used for taking a reality check of an IT project? What model could be used to bridge the jargon gap in conversation with technical persons? What model would generally parallel most of the activities of the SDP, from the identification of requirements to final delivery and acceptance of the system? What model, familiar to everyone, would address the issues of quality trade-offs and cost-benefit analysis? What model would be complex enough not to be dismissed as irrelevant and overly simplistic? What model would be nonthreatening and even fun to work with?

A Model Framework to Promote Communication

Underlying the entire discussion that follows is the premise that any complex development or engineering project has analogies. In 1987, John Zachman published an article in the *IBM Systems Journal* entitled "A Framework for Information Systems Architecture." Zachman noted that discussions about systems development efforts quickly get to the guru-quoting and dictionary-citing phase. Not only is it difficult to get agreement about a general topic of development, but there is often complete disagreement over terminology, phase, and scope. Thus, progress stalls.

Originally written for IT professionals, the goal of Zachman's article was to improve communications between technical team members during a systems development project. Zachman found it useful to temporarily ignore the language of data processing and look to the field of architecture. He borrowed the construction business' concepts about how to manage complex development efforts and, by analogy, applied them to information systems development. In this way, communications between team members improved.

Business managers attempting to get value and quality for their technology dollar can certainly use this same analogy to improve their understanding and control of an IT project. By using the similar, but neutral, process of construction, business managers can evaluate the depth and breadth of an IT provider's understanding and application of the SDP on a development effort. It may be discovered that some IT providers do not subscribe to the discipline of the SDP or perhaps aren't even aware of the sequence of its execution. By understanding the close parallels between the steps of construction and the process of systems development, business managers are in a much better position to estimate the probable success or failure of any automation project, and can take corrective action as necessary.

By requiring the full and uncompromising execution of each SDP phase, business managers can significantly raise the probability of success. Without full execution of the SDP, the chance of failure is heightened, with cost overruns and schedule delays being guaranteed.

The first figure in chapters 5–9 portrays, side-by-side, the phases of a construction project with the phases of the SDP. Activities listed are for comparison purposes, so that similarities can be seen. Discussion of each figure and phase conveys the following:

- IT projects are complex and require the active participation of business managers to be successful.
- IT projects intimately affect the way business is conducted, and they must be carefully defined, designed, and constructed.
- IT projects use different skills at different times and must be thoroughly planned, managed, and coordinated.
- Sufficient time must be spent in defining business requirements so that late and expensive changes to the technology system are minimized.
- IT projects have a technical and a workplace component. The workplace component can only be established and implemented by workplace managers. The technical component must fit smoothly into the workplace component (see Figure 1.3).
- Technology must be designed to enhance the work process activities of employees. If not, negative side effects may irritate or inconvenience customers and overstress employees.

Additionally, Figures 5.1, 6.1, 7.1, 8.1, and 9.1 reference QM principles from chapter 3. These should be consciously applied during the activities of that phase. Use of these principles at the appropriate time can help ensure the quality needed to maximize the benefit from the technology investment and deliver a system that adds real value to the business while reducing project risk.

The Conceptual Phase

The initial period of any new project is marked with high enthusiasm and a desire for the best. This period characteristically involves many ideas that have gathered over time. With the example of home construction, potential house buyers have been gathering and are influenced by many books, magazines, real estate newspaper sections, and discussions with friends and acquaintances. They are greatly influenced by marketing sources of information, and unless they are professional developers, they have a less-than-professional knowledge of the degree of complexity and difficulty involved in the actual construction of homes. House buyers are likely to have a concept of the dream home that is a composite of many different constructed models to which they have been exposed (Figure 5.1). Living areas, baths, bedrooms, and amenities are often viewed out of context with any overall building plan and are visualized almost as if they stand alone. It is also a common fact that the concept of the dream home often exceeds one's ability to pay, since the house does not fit into any overall financial plan. Certain future financial obligations exist and the dream home is one of these, but rarely are the costs associated with actual construction fully understood. It is easy to underestimate the cumulative financial burden to which house buyers are ultimately subjecting themselves. The reality of being house poor is often the result of proceeding on a project without full understanding of the likelihood of cost overruns and the effect these have on all other financial aspects. Specifically, home buyers fail to appreciate the reality of *creeping featurism* (that is, little enhancements here and there). Thus, the dilemma they face, when behind schedule, is that a little more money and time will make it right.

But these issues are not thought of during the conceptual phase, driven as it is by dreams and enthusiasm. House buyers may know enough to know what they don't know; and they do know enough not to proceed without additional knowledge and assistance.

Business managers in today's computerized world are faced with a similar situation. Information and communication technologies are changing the way business is conducted, and the rate of change is increasing rapidly. Economic factors and competitive realities are convincing business owners that they need to do things differently and that the technolo-

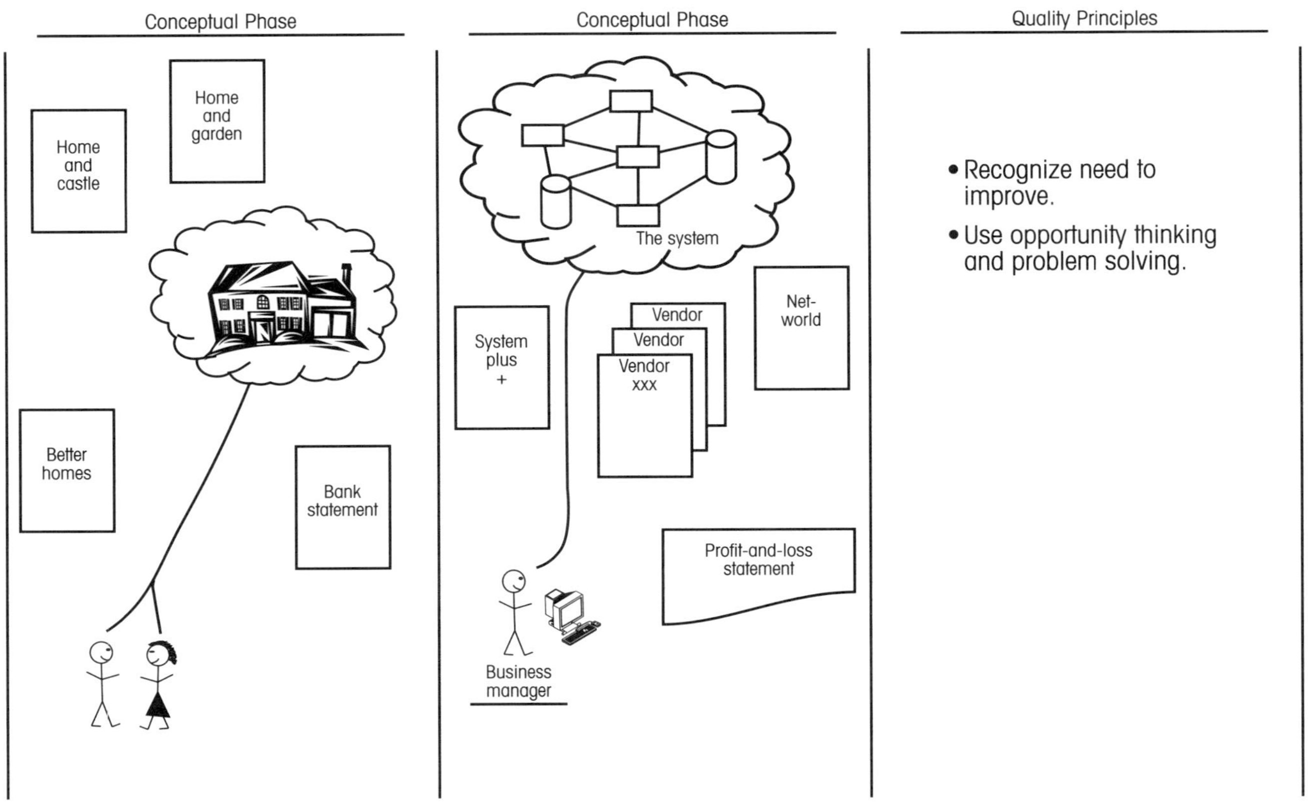

- Recognize need to improve.
- Use opportunity thinking and problem solving.

Figure 5.1. The conceptual phase.

gies of automation somehow play into this change. Everywhere business managers look, they see the touted benefits of technology and are left with the impression that their operation would be much more efficient, effective, and profitable if automated. Just as future home owners conceptualize a more desirable dwelling, business managers begin to conceptualize a better, cheaper, and more modern way of doing business. In some cases, this vision originates with the financial manager, because the claims of cost savings through automation fit nicely with certain economic goals of the business. In other cases, the vision may emanate from employees, experienced with personal computers, who see a brighter future in more technology.

However the vision is created, the sources of information providing input to the concept can be overwhelming with regard to the actual technologies that could be used in bringing the concept to reality. As noted, staying current and proficient with these technologies and their application is a nearly impossible task even for technologists. How can business managers hope to cope?! Yet many try.

The parallels between conceptualizing a custom house and an automated business support system are similar. Each requires the expertise of specialists and the discipline of proven methods of construction. Each requires an analysis of needs and desires to assure realism of project goals and the sufficiency of budget and time to finish the project.

Before proceeding to a discussion of the requirements definition phase, there is a need to see how the home construction example would change if a predesigned/modular (track) house were chosen. With regards to the business IT project, the difference lies with the use of off-the-shelf software systems versus those specifically designed and built for a business' needs.

In each case, decisions must be made concerning the appropriateness or *fit* of this track house versus that track house or this off-the-shelf system versus that off-the-shelf system. Decisions of this type must be made with full knowledge of the requirements to be satisfied; the limitations and constraints of the various track homes or off-the-shelf systems; an identification of the requirements not satisfied; and the extent and cost of modifications to the track home or off-the-shelf system to satisfy those requirements.

This is an area of special vulnerability for business managers faced with the challenge of automating an activity. Off-the-shelf systems have certain advantages and are heavily marketed. They also have inherent disadvantages (that is, unanticipated changes to business work processes or customer service) that must be fully understood and considered. If the goal of automating a business activity is to realize increased efficiencies and improved customer service, then the capabilities and limitations attendant with an off-the-shelf system must be understood and carefully compensated for when implemented in the actual workplace. Experience has shown that implementations of reasonably priced, off-the-shelf solutions usually cost many times the initial purchase price when modified for use in the real world of a particular business.

This issue is mentioned here in a cautionary vein. It is extremely easy to read into marketing materials and vendor presentations a scope of functionality and ease of implementation for an off-the-shelf system that simply don't exist. An informed decision can proceed only after a clear understanding of the requirements that the off-the-shelf solution is supposed to satisfy.

Additionally, trade-offs occur with mass-produced items to make them competitive and affordable. Those trade-offs may result in a less-than-satisfying solution for the business' automation challenge.

Requirements Definition

Without a doubt, the most critical phase in house construction is the period of time spent in defining the dwelling's requirements. Only after these are identified and confirmed by the buyer can architects begin to intelligently design a house that meets those requirements. But determining them is a difficult process unless money is not a consideration. When money is no object, all wants, needs, and desires can be considered equally important and be treated as design specifications. Only when two requirements structurally compete, must a compromise be reached.

Usually, however, money is a primary constraint, and the objective is to get the greatest value for the buyer's dollar. In this case, wants and desires must be considered separate from needs inasmuch as needs represent a minimum baseline of housing below which the buyer cannot go

(Figure 5.2). Only after this minimum level has been determined should wants and desires be entertained. Rarely can this analysis be accomplished without a knowledge of housing design and construction. Enter the architect! He or she not only brings knowledge and expertise to the scene, but, more importantly, provides a forum within which the determination of requirements can occur. This is an interactive dialogue where needs, wants, and desires, quality, time frames, and costs are traded off in an attempt to assist buyers in making decisions concerning exactly what they expect to see built and at what cost.

The architect is also responsible to bring knowledge of the requirements of certain interested and external parties to the house construction. Specifically, the architect is expected to apply all building and environmental code requirements to the chosen design, so that such requirements are satisfied in the final building, and it passes all necessary inspections.

The work product of the requirements definition phase is a clear statement of the dwelling's essential features accompanied by a prioritized list of desirable features. Affordability is also determined and the likelihood that financing can be arranged.

The architect has been essential in bringing a semblance of order to the rather open-ended conceptualization of the previous phase. Without the architect, the critical skills of applying knowledge of construction to the needs and desires of the future home owners would have been absent. In this absence, the owners would have been at a decided disadvantage in moving their project forward. Their ability to make informed trade-offs within the knowledge of sound construction practices would be limited. Also, their understanding of what can be reasonably expected of a construction contractor could seriously hamper them in the upcoming phases, where extreme specificity is critical to contracting and actual construction.

Applying IT to business processes is no less complex; and the need for the equivalent of an architect is no less urgent. The business managers' difficulty is to know when, indeed, an equivalent is present. In the world of information technology, the architect's equal would be the kind of systems analyst discussed in chapter 4. As noted, however, the title *sys-*

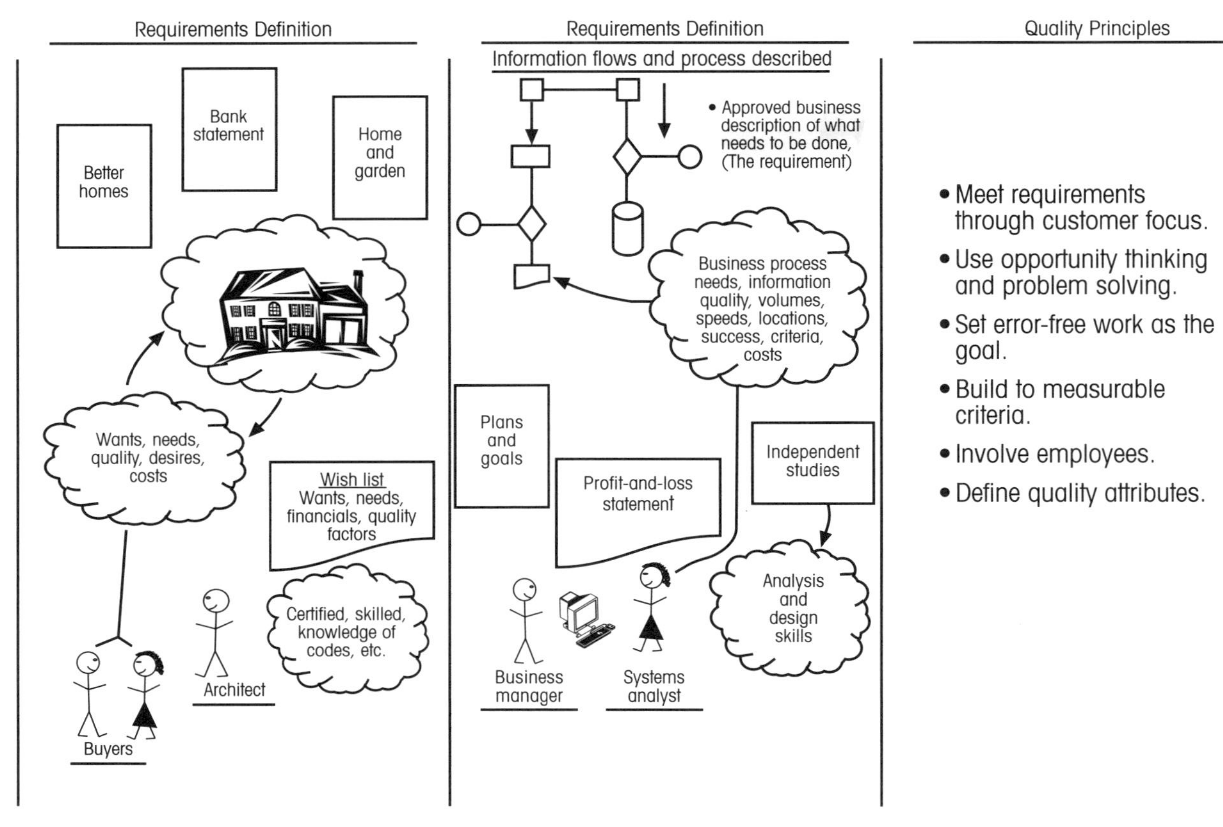

Figure 5.2. Requirements definition.

tems analyst can mean a great many things. Business managers must be very specific as to the functions the analyst is to perform in this early stage of the project. As it progresses, different kinds of analysts may be employed to study specific components of the overall system. For example, a certain database structure may seem appropriate for a business need, but it will probably require an analyst proficient in the workings of that type of structure and in various vendor renditions of that structure to ensure a successful design and working implementation.

For now the need is quite simple. Business managers need to work with unbiased systems analysts on how to best bring automation to the business. By unbiased it is meant that this architect/analyst represents no particular vendor and advocates no particular technical solutions. The analyst is an experienced IT generalist and is motivated to solve the business problem or exploit added-value opportunities using the most effective methods that have been proven to work. This person performs the function of taking the high-level conceptualization of the business managers through an analysis that proposes several ways to meet the business goal within the realities of contemporary technology offerings. As noted, the architect/analyst's method of consultation should embody the counsel of Hippocrates to first do no harm. This consultation facilitates the managers' thinking through the implications of the conceptualization. In accomplishing this, good analysts can, at times, be viewed as irritants. They are forever asking questions that seem far removed from computers, software, and networks.

These questions seek to uncover the processing requirements in business terms, information needs, levels of desired information quality, speeds, volumes, locations, and plans for expansion and growth. There may even be queries concerning the amount of money available for the project. Thus, the analyst attempts to determine if the conceptualization for automation is well founded; not in the sense of questioning business plans and justifications, but in the sense of whether or not affordable automation is likely to add real value to the business operation. This architect/analyst needs as complete a picture of the business as possible, so that risks can be minimized and expectations kept reasonable. This analyst recognizes that business managers are in the vulnerable position where unrealistic IT expectations, budgets, and schedules can lead a business into dangerous ground and can jeopardize careers.

The architect/analyst also attempts to determine the degree of technological sophistication that can be reasonably handled by the existing workforce. Figure 3.1 is the principal model used at this time, since determining all elements of development and user readiness for automation is a great concern.

Like the architect, the systems analyst is attempting to separate wants and desires from essential business needs and realities from wishes. Knowing that business managers may have already been influenced by vendors, marketing materials, or less-experienced internal experts, the analyst attempts—through dialogue about requirements and through education—to assist business managers in understanding that care must be exercised in making decisions concerning implementation of the conceptualized system. This analyst does not force a predetermined solution onto the problem or opportunity, but knows that the best possible solution can be determined by continuing to pursue the analysis in a disciplined and comprehensive fashion. The analyst believes in a studied approach similar to that outlined in this book and will attempt to convey the reasonableness of this approach to business managers. To the extent that business managers buy into this deliberate approach, this initial phase will be a success with real and necessary requirements being identified. If this approach is not adopted by managers, the architect/analyst will likely explain the risks inherent in making technology decisions without proper analysis and excuse him or herself from the project. If objectivity and candor do not seem important to business managers, this analyst will know that the chances for success just plummeted and may withdraw from the project.

Quality Principles Employed

The systems analyst, functioning as architect, is primarily concerned with obtaining a clear understanding of what business managers need to accomplish. From this baseline, the analyst proceeds to think in terms of processes for satisfying the business requirement. In order to do this, heavy involvement by customer representatives is required as both technical and nontechnical aspects of the work process are designed to be error-free. Figures 1.1 and 4.1 guide this analysis to ensure that IT is not an imposition on the workplace and its employees. This focus on the customer helps to guarantee that overall workplace effectiveness is achieved, thus promoting improved business processing quality.

This approach is in stark contrast to many previous applications of technology where employees in the workplace were often an afterthought. This approach, combined with the work of the business' existing QM action teams, can often introduce opportunities and ways to exploit technologies not thought of by management. Thus, employee involvement can result in breakthroughs that often give the business a new competitive edge.

By far the most important QM activity conducted during requirements analysis is the need to define the quality attributes for both the processing system and the information products resulting from the systems operation. In chapter 1, it was seen that the information requirements need to be described using quality attribute and system performance terminology. Table 5.1 lists common system quality and performance attributes with acceptable ways of measurement.

Most of these attributes, such as accuracy, need to be described in measurable terms that are determined by business usage. For example, the response time of an employee at a terminal to answer a customer's query could easily, without proper analysis, be stated in either unrealistically fast or slow terms. The first tendency is to state that an immediate response time is needed, not realizing the extreme expense incurred if the word *immediate* was actually used as a design criterion for the system. Too slow, on the other hand, will increase the business risk of customer irritation and employee inattention and boredom.

From a practical standpoint, each quality and performance attribute found in Table 5.1 needs to be examined from the perspective of how important each is to the business process being automated. To achieve this, business managers will likely confer with other members of the management team such as the auditor and perhaps the security administrators. Without such definition, the technologist is left to guess what is important and how quality and performance elements impact the

Table 5.1. Quality attributes.

Attributes	Ways to define and measure
Accurate	• Absolute values • Within range • Reasonableness • Consistent
Timely	• Decision/action cycles • Reporting cycles • Process sequences • Real-time defined
Reliable	• Mean time between failures (MTBF) • Reporting cycles • Number of complaints • Number of errors • Degree of trust
Auditable	• Reconstruction processes • Compliance with account standards • Traceability of transactions
Secured	• Access controls • Breaches of confidentiality
Simplicity	• Understandable by user • Technical writer input
Testable	• Conformance to expected outputs • Demonstrable and monitored • Meaningful to someone else
Documented	• For training • For maintenance • For operations • Standard formats

business. This is too much discretion to allow the technologist. Either the guess will not be stringent enough, and the final system will not exhibit the required degrees of quality and performance; or the guess will be unnecessarily demanding, and systems costs will be higher than required.

From a QM perspective, great attention and dialogue must be given to this issue of determining which quality attributes are important and how they will be measured. Without this criterion, the analysts and managers cannot intelligently proceed to the next phase of development. They will be caught trying to design and construct a system against a shifting background of what seems to satisfy the business requirement. Continual changes during construction will be needed and at greater cost than if determined early in the requirements definition phase.

Referring again to Figure 1.3, it must be remembered that the use of technology needs to be accomplished with full consideration given to the nontechnical aspects of the business process. Changes brought by automation to nontechnical work processes must be completely understood. With this knowledge, the systems analyst, acting as an architect, can proceed to propose alternative ways to use automation and relate such use to the basic work process affected.

Summary

At the conclusion of the requirements definition phase, the architect/analyst must have a clear and documented understanding of the desired improvements to the work process. These should not be vague statements about increasing profits and productivity or improving customer service. That was adequate during the conceptualization phase, but not now! Requirements need to be crisp work process statements described in terms of measurable quality attributes and performance. In the language of QM, these statements form the basis for doing right things (DRT). In the next phase of development, alternative analysis and feasibility study, this understanding of DRT undergoes further definition and refinement, as specific alternatives for meeting the requirements are proposed and studied. So, it is critical that the statement of requirements be as clear as possible by the end of the requirements phase, otherwise much of the effort in devising and articulating alternative ways of meeting the requirements is wasted.

CHAPTER 6

Automating the Business Requirement (Part 2): Alternatives Analysis Phase

Alternatives Analysis and Feasibility Study

While often slighted, this phase is essential for deciding what direction a construction project should take. This phase establishes a set of parameters within which the complexities of home construction can proceed. First, the architect takes all requirements (wants and needs) from the previous conceptual and requirements definition phase and formulates various possibilities for the home buyers. In doing this, the architect balances requirements against the home buyers' financial situation. In proposing different possibilities, the architect brings knowledge and experience to the effort that most buyers do not have. For example, the architect possesses knowledge of construction, model types, materials, and sources of supply; the prevailing cost trends of the local construction industry; the reputation of contractors; sources of financing; and the building codes of oversight jurisdictions. The architect also contributes the explicit obligations of being a licensed professional with a code of ethics (Figure 6.1).

By proposing alternative solutions to the identified housing requirements, the architect and buyers can continue the dialogue and refine what the buyers need and desire. Together, they can determine a likely way the buyers can be satisfied given all the competing factors. It is a time for honest discussion about trade-offs and for realism. It is the first time that expectations can be tempered and brought into line with what the buyers can afford and how long it may take for delivery.

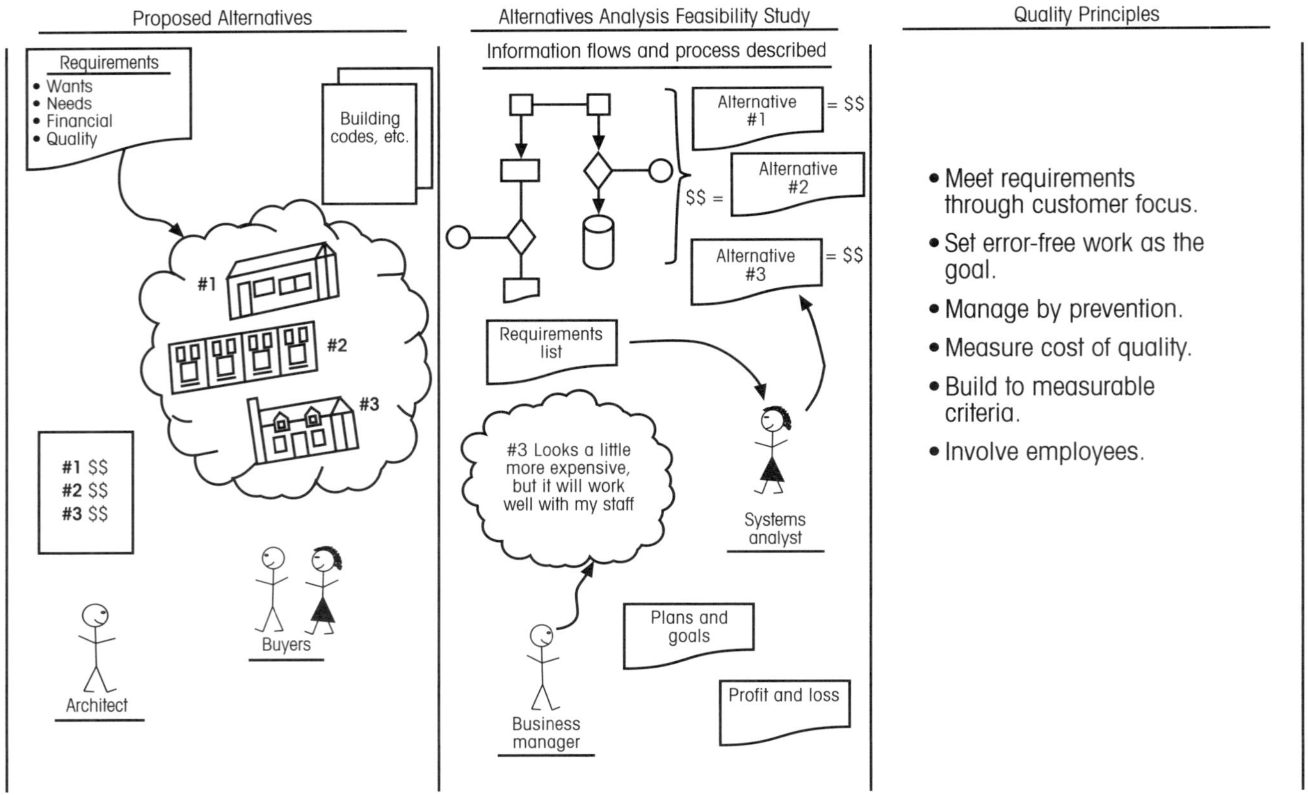

Figure 6.1. Alternatives analysis and feasibility study.

The architect may submit several alternative proposals, each seeking to satisfy all essential housing needs while attempting to meet as many of the buyers' nonessential desires as possible. Also with these proposals, different levels of quality (for example, gold versus brass faucets) for certain features can be traded off against other features within the buyers' financial limits. During this process, however, the architect will guard against the compromise of essential housing needs through the acquisition of frivolous features. For each proposal, high-level drawings are prepared depicting the physical layout of the structure. These drawings are not detailed enough to proceed with construction, but they are specific enough to generate reasonably accurate cost data for planning purposes.

The architect attempts to obtain the buyers' acceptance of a proposal as soon as possible, so that actual detailed design can begin. To delay too long is to risk loss of the architect to another project and the need to redo all cost estimates because of changing construction conditions and inflation. A conscientious architect will discuss with the buyer the importance of the decision regarding proposal selection and will stress the consequences of increased budget and schedule estimates should changes be made later during construction. While some flexibility exists, the basic construction design needs to be frozen.

For business managers facing IT decisions, the situation, while essentially the same, is considerably more complex. To begin with, everyone can conceive of the activities associated with constructing a house; not so when bringing IT to a business process. As noted, the complexities of computers are not apparent to those uninitiated in the technology, and there is no other technology that creates such dependencies and far-reaching impacts on a business. For these reasons, the exploration of alternatives and their feasibility is necessary. While searching for alternative ways to satisfy the requirements, the architect/analyst continues the definition of system requirements by presenting nontechnical managers with specific automated proposals and operational scenarios. Each of these alternatives (usually there are two or three, formulated from the analyst's understanding of the business need) allows business managers to determine the analyst's grasp of that need. It also allows business managers to reaffirm their own understanding of the need.

The architect/analyst knows that the definition of requirements is not a one-time thing. That is, it is an iterative process that must culminate in a statement of need that is sufficiently clear, concise, and factual to allow the analyst to proceed with the most appropriate design. Further, the analyst knows that in arriving at the most appropriate solution, each alternative is subjected to a series of feasibility and trade-off tests that examine each alternative according to technical, operational, and economic factors. If diligently conducted, these feasibility tests identify the best possible alternative. The recommended sequence for performing the feasibility tests follows.

Technical Feasibility

Technical feasibility examines each proposed alternative solution to determine a number of important issues. Does the solution employ a reliable use of technology or new and relatively untried methods, hardware, software, and processing techniques? In my experience, the more a technical solution is promoted in the commercial systems news media, the less tested it probably is and the higher the risk in using it.

The technical solution should be straightforward. There should be very few unanswered questions as to how it will work and how it will be supported within the business environment.

There should be a stable source of trained personnel in the information industry's workforce capable of implementing the contemplated approach. The more esoteric the technical solution, the fewer people who can understand it and the higher their price tag. Also, the threat of being held hostage by a unique and nonstandard solution must be avoided.

If the technical solution is to be maintained by inhouse system employees, it must be compatible with their basic skills. Learning a software package is one thing; learning a new architectural approach to processing is quite another (for example, going from batch processing to a client/server environment).

The technical solution should not overly tax the capabilities of mainline workplace employees. Remember, the system is supposed to make them more effective and efficient, not less.

Finally, does a structured training curriculum for obtaining the basic computer skills needed for systems maintenance and operation exist? This could be a combination of local community college education offerings and system provider training. If basic training has to be developed especially for a business, reconsider this alternative. Training issues and the ability to equip employees to successfully use the IT system lie at the heart of the next test of feasibility.

Operational Feasibility

Operational feasibility is the most often overlooked aspect of deciding an automated course of action. Yet it is the most critical.

Operational feasibility seeks to determine how well each technical alternative will play in the business' day-to-day operating environment. What is desired is an application of technology that enhances performance in some specific way and is not in any way disruptive. This means that the workplace procedures currently in force must be appropriately changed to accommodate the technology. This must be recognized and planned for early in the project. All too often a misunderstanding exists that these procedural changes are somehow being made by the developer responsible for the technical portions of the overall system. This is usually not the case.

These operational aspects include all the factors on the right side of Figure 1.3 (page 3). These social and organizational elements must be taken into account during this step of the feasibility study. It is common, if too little attention is given to actual operational considerations, to have sophisticated and elegant technical systems thrust on a workforce not adequately prepared to assimilate them. Or, as is even more common, such systems are not comprehensively tested under realistic conditions and prove disruptive to operations when put into widespread use.

Each technical alternative should be analyzed to determine its impact on the social and organizational elements of work. While it is understood and desired that automation changes the ways in which business is conducted; it is the business managers' judgment call as to how much and how fast the workplace can absorb such change. To help make this judgment call, the following should be considered.

- Assess the current level of customer satisfaction. Take care not to risk good existing relations with unproven technology.
- Determine the competitors' technologies. Don't risk market share and satisfied customers unless there is a clear advantage in doing so. Be careful not to put at risk any core business proficiency while pursuing a new technology and its promise of new and different business opportunities.
- Factor into the evaluation all changes required to absorb each technical alternative smoothly. These are the changes that the workforce and workplace will encounter in operating the alternative.
- Consider employees' sophistication level with regard to technology. Too much too soon can result in disaster.
- Factor into the project's budget adequate training dollars. In 1991, Paul Straussman, former Assistant Secretary of Defense for Information Systems, U.S. Department of Defense, estimated $2 to $3 of training for each dollar spent on hardware and software. No one can afford the business that is lost while employees try to figure out the system by practicing on customers.
- Factor in dollars for contract maintenance support or for in-house systems personnel to be trained to take on maintenance.
- Determine the ease of expanding each proposed technical alternative to meet expected business growth.
- Evaluate the capability of local area system providers to continue support of each technical alternative if necessary.
- Determine the adequacy of systems documentation. In-house maintenance personnel require far greater levels of detail than if contract support is used. Documentation represents the blue prints and engineering drawings of the system and are absolutely essential for maintenance and eventual upgrades.

It is important to dampen enthusiasm and be a little skeptical during the operational feasibility analysis; especially since technological proponents will be pushing hard for their favored alternative. The architect/

analyst assisting business managers with these evaluations should continue to be objective, caring only for the welfare of the business. An experienced analyst will stress the liveability of each alternative, letting the business managers conclude what is best for operational success.

Having determined which technical alternatives are operationally feasible, attention turns to the economics of automation.

Economic Feasibility

Economic feasibility should be considered last or else the probability is high that the business' technological direction could be determined for the wrong reason; that is, low cost. Since the actual hardware and software components are only a partial means to an end (that is, improved quality and performance of a business work process), the totality of that work process must be considered. This was accomplished through the operational feasibility analysis.

Of course, any decision to expend dollars on technology is usually justified to the financial manager through the identification of increased revenues, reduced costs, or new and better services designed to retain customers and grow market share. Benefits from the use of technology can only be estimated after an examination of the overall work process being modified by automation. Thus, the following questions must be asked: Will the benefits from a technical and operationally feasible alternative come through

- Reduced overhead or production costs? How measured?
- Increased productivity and/or profit? How measured?
- Improved customer service for competitive reasons?
- New business products and services through better use of information?
- Increased sales through better use of marketing data?

Over the last three decades, the economic justification for most business IT investments has been to claim a reduction in overhead and operating costs. This has usually been translated into a reduction in employees. But this rationale, as a continuing justification for future technological investments, is beginning to be questioned. Some are starting to wonder at the long-term wisdom of continuing to eliminate middle management and even clerical personnel on the assumption that IT systems will not only pick up the slack, but also will significantly improve productivity. Peter Drucker (1992) has some interesting observations on the wisdom of this approach in his book *Managing for the Future*. Drucker doubts whether any actual improvement has been experienced in the white-collar arena; and this after over 20 years of automating administrative and management work functions. One of the more serious difficulties appears to be that organizations, through excessive reductions in midlevel employees and managers, are losing their corporate memory. Now, it could be argued that in this fast-moving technological age of the downsized organization, corporate memories tend to tie employees to the old ways. At the same time, it must be remembered that while all this exciting and innovative reengineering and reinventing is going on, the organization—like it or not—is probably going to remain dependent on old systems developed many years ago. In many cases these systems are well into their second decade of use. The wrong personnel reductions or too many reductions can threaten the viability of these systems. Often the basic misunderstanding of what people do and what computers are supposed to do exists. This can lead to false and dangerous economies (Figure 1.1).

This is why technical and operational feasibility were first examined. Care must be taken to conduct the economic analysis only on alternatives that will work smoothly, with as little initial disruption as possible. Without this assurance, a favorable economic analysis of a too-disruptive alternative could condemn the business to a situation where potential benefits and profits are overwhelmed by the unanticipated costs associated with making the system work. (Here, *favorable* is used in the sense that most economic analyzes cannot adequately take into account the intangible factors negatively affecting the workforce or customers.) This all-too-common experience accounts for the 40 percent marginal score reflected in Figure 1.2. So it is imperative that business managers be reasonably certain of the liveability of the technical proposals subjected to economic analysis.

To get a true picture of the cost aspects of an IT system, the elements of Table 6.1 should be estimated for each alternative and entered on the cost side of an economic analysis evaluation.

Be sure that each cost item is addressed and that all blanks are explained as to why they don't apply to the alternative under analysis. Typical cost item estimates and justifications cover only a small portion of the items reflected in the table. Many technologists supply only hardware and software estimates and only for the acquisition and operating phases; that is, the upper left portion of the table. By doing so, they fail to acknowledge as much as two-thirds of the total cost of a system over its useful life span. This may be a reason why IT managers in large corporations tend to have credibility problems with other corporate executives. The reasons for submitting incomplete cost item estimates vary from ignorance to salesmanship to the excuse, We'll worry about that later!

It should be readily apparent that benefits, to offset such costs, must be sizeable. It should also be evident that many of the cost items reflect a need for in-house or contract support expertise, which may, in the long run, be more expensive than laying off employees and reporting it as a cost savings on the benefit's side of the spreadsheet.

For an IT effort to be successful, it must be funded and justified by enough offsetting benefits to allow it to stay the developmental course through to operations and beyond. This means that projected benefits over the useful life of the system—a difficult estimation to make—must more than cover all of the pertinent costs seen in Table 6.1. A weak benefits analysis subjects the development effort to constant pressure to show something soon for the money. On the other hand, initiatives that are well founded in actual business process improvements and good costing tend to have realistic benefit projections and enjoy the patience of users and management as the development progresses.

The alternative that has passed all three tests of feasibility will be easy to explain and easy to defend unless the assumptions underlying the initiative have changed. If new or changed assumptions or new requirements surface, it is imperative to revisit each feasibility test for each proposed alternative.

Table 6.1. Items to consider in cost analysis.

	Acquisition costs	Operating costs	Upgrade costs
Hardware equipment	Equipment installation	Maintenance/ warranty Annual lease/rental	Hardware replacement or upgrades
Software	Software One-time license Initial charges	Annual licensing Maintenance fees Warranty	Software replacement or upgrades
Personnel	Recruiting Training and education Planning, design, and selection Hardware and software programming Contract	Routine monitoring and operations Problem determination and correction User liaison and administration Programming maintenance	User changes Software changes and upgrades Training and education Programming Contract programming
Communications	Initial hookup	Monthly tariffs Hookup Security Tariffs	Additional lines and equipment
Facilities	Facilities development Wiring Security Plumbing	Floor space Power Air cooling Security	Incremental wiring Incremental space Increased security

Additional Feasibility Tests

There are three additional areas that, while included in the traditional tests of feasibility, need to be examined separately because their impact is so great. These are performance, internal control and security, and service/efficiency.

Performance

Performance problems occur when business tasks are done too slowly to achieve objectives. Performance opportunities often occur when the use of technology speeds up a business task even though it is achieving the objective. Performance with IT systems is usually measured by throughput and response time. *Throughput* is the amount of work performed over a defined period of time. *Response time* is the delay between the entry of a transaction into the system and a response to that transaction. As long as the fundamental business tasks are not adversely affected by the speedup, new and faster technological upgrades can be periodically employed to provide improved efficiencies. Care must be taken, however, to ensure that brute speedups actually improve employee job performance and do not end up resembling Lucy and Ethel in the famous chocolate candy assembly line scene from *I Love Lucy!* Note that although throughput and response time can be considered separately, they should also be considered together.

Internal Controls and Security

Controls and security lend accuracy, stability, and reliability to the IT business processing environment. Internal controls and security must be balanced against throughput and response time. A system with too few controls will eventually result in discrepancies between what the IT system says is real and what is actually going on in the business. Controls are needed to ensure the accuracy of information and the integrity of the business process. Without internal controls, it is common to experience the slow corruption of corporate recordkeeping. Also, systems with too few controls are open to fraudulent manipulation and abusive practices.

But it is possible to go overboard! Too many controls, checks, and balances slow response time and throughput. Decisions concerning this balancing act must be made by business managers, auditors, lawyers, and security administrators—not the technologists.

Security is concerned with the control of access to sensitive business information and other proprietary or sensitive data pertaining to customers and clients. Certain privacy laws carry penalties for breaches of confidentiality. The unauthorized release of proprietary client data will certainly result in a lawsuit. Security has also evolved to be concerned with the proper backup of software and information and the ability to survive outages and recover rapidly. To deal with these special concerns, the architect/analyst may suggest additional outside consultation in helping business managers select the most feasible alternative.

Efficiency and Service

An efficiency analysis can be confused with the economic test of feasibility. While economy is concerned with the amount of resources used to get a specific benefit or payback; efficiency is concerned with the use of those resources with a minimum of waste. Efficiency is closely related to the concept of cost of quality. Quality of an information system, as has been seen, is measured by how well the system's outputs contribute to or detract from the quality of the work process outputs that the system supports. The degree of efficiency involved in producing a quality information product or service is directly related to the design of the proposed alternatives. A well-designed information system anticipates a wide range of potential errors that could occur during all steps of processing and will trap and reconcile these errors early in the process, where the cost to fix them is lowest (Figure 3.2). This efficiency is key to obtaining the projected economic benefits of the system. It also prevents adverse customer reactions should errors adversely affect their business transactions.

Design shortcuts taken in the error detection and processing aspect of the information system should be avoided at all costs. Remember also that the system covers all elements of the workplace environment and requires the direct involvement of nontechnical managers to ensure an operationally acceptable solution to error processing.

A service analysis is triggered by the desire to improve service to internal system users, to external customers, or to both. Service improvements are often the first quality enhancements identified during a system analysis. Like the other categories in this discussion, service improvements may be intended to solve specific, identified problems; exploit chances to improve service; or satisfy some management mandate.

The performance of a service analysis of a proposed systems alternative requires that

- An identified and measurable set of service objectives exist from the previous requirement analysis. These objectives could be to

  —Improve accuracy.

  —Increase reliability.

  —Improve ease of use.

  —Enhance throughput or response time.

  Each of these service objectives find their origins and justification in the problem or opportunity analysis of the previous phase of development and have been expressed as quality attributes.
- The customers and/or users of the system support and agree with the service objectives.
- The nontechnical workplace aspects of the system's environment have been addressed, and the supporting social and organizations aspects of the improvements are planned.

It is important that service improvement expectations be realistic. They should be based on actual analysis and not the vague promises of marketing brochures. Finally, it must be remembered that the solution to one problem may, in fact, become a problem unto itself.

Quality Principles Employed

The most critical QM principle for this phase remains customer focus. It is only through continued dialogue about requirements that a clear understanding of the final system can be formed. The process of alternatives analysis is primarily an effort to further refine customer requirements by offering models, mock-ups, and prototype solutions that meet the requirements as the architect/analyst understands them. It is the business managers' responsibility to participate in the review of these alternatives. The tests of feasibility are a form of preventive thinking, in that they pose questions that deal with practicality and measurable operational realities. If taken seriously, the tests of feasibility, by eliminating impractical and unrealistic solutions, can lead to system designs that promote error-free work. Progressing to the next stage of development (design) with an unrealistic and infeasible solution guarantees outright failure of the effort, or, as is more common, the excessively expensive and disruptive jerry-rigging of ill-fitting equipment, software, and processes that actually impedes the business, loses customers, and adversely affects employees.

Note also, that the tests of feasibility can reduce total systems development and operational costs by ensuring that all participants are reasonably certain as to what is being built. The elimination of errors and omissions in requirements, as well as misunderstandings arising from needs versus desires, means that the amount of waste, scrap, and rework during construction is minimized. In this way, the ultimate cost of quality is kept low.

Summary

The alternatives analysis phase is important for several reasons. First, with proposed alternative ways to satisfy the business processing requirements, business managers can make informed decisions regarding a course of action. Without alternatives analysis, there is only one course of action, that being the one favored by the most vocal proponent. It may well be the best way to proceed but business managers will never know for sure since no comparison, except against the current system, is made.

Second, alternatives analysis is important because the critical interplay and trade-offs among technical, operational, and economic factors can be analyzed. Third, the decision from the analysis of alternatives commits the business to a development and implementation path that can be both expensive and difficult to retreat from as the company proceeds.

It is imperative to stop, look, and listen with the architect/analyst to the thought process and results of an alternatives analysis. Finally, the analysis may inform nontechnical managers that an automated solution is not needed or not appropriate at this time. Often, it is better to do nothing rather than to proceed down an ill-defined or vaguely justified path.

These first three stages of house construction or systems development allow all parties to arrive at a clear, concise, and agreed-upon description of what is to be built and delivered.

In the next chapter, the question of design is addressed. Integral to the design is the sequencing of implementation actions. Depending on the complexity of the system chosen, different deployment strategies exist. Regardless of strategy, however, the expectations of users, customers, managers, and even developers need to be closely monitored so that compatibility is maintained with the delivered system. Managing expectations is critical to successful system development efforts.

CHAPTER 7

Automating the Business Requirement (Part 3): Design Phase

Analysis and Design

In the initial stages of the house-building project, the principal function of the architect is consultive. The importance of progressing from enthusiastic conceptualization to realistic expectations cannot be overemphasized. If the buyers' view of the constructed house remains fanciful and untempered by an analysis of what is feasible, then no clear agreement exists between architect and buyers, because no common goal has been established. The first three phases of the development process exist for the purpose of defining, and then refining, not only the overall design of the house, but the assumptions and constraints under which it will be constructed, financed, and delivered.

During this, the design phase, major resource expenditures begin. So, once again, it must be stated that success, from this point on, is greatly dependent on keeping changes to a minimum. The uncertainties associated with such projects should, as much as possible, lie beyond the buyers (Figure 7.1). Unless absolutely necessary, change should be eliminated from the buyers' thinking. Even minor changes can have disastrous effects on delivery schedules and resource utilization levels. For these reasons, the house construction must proceed from a stable set of requirements and from the analyzed and agreed-upon, high-level design of the chosen, feasible alternative.

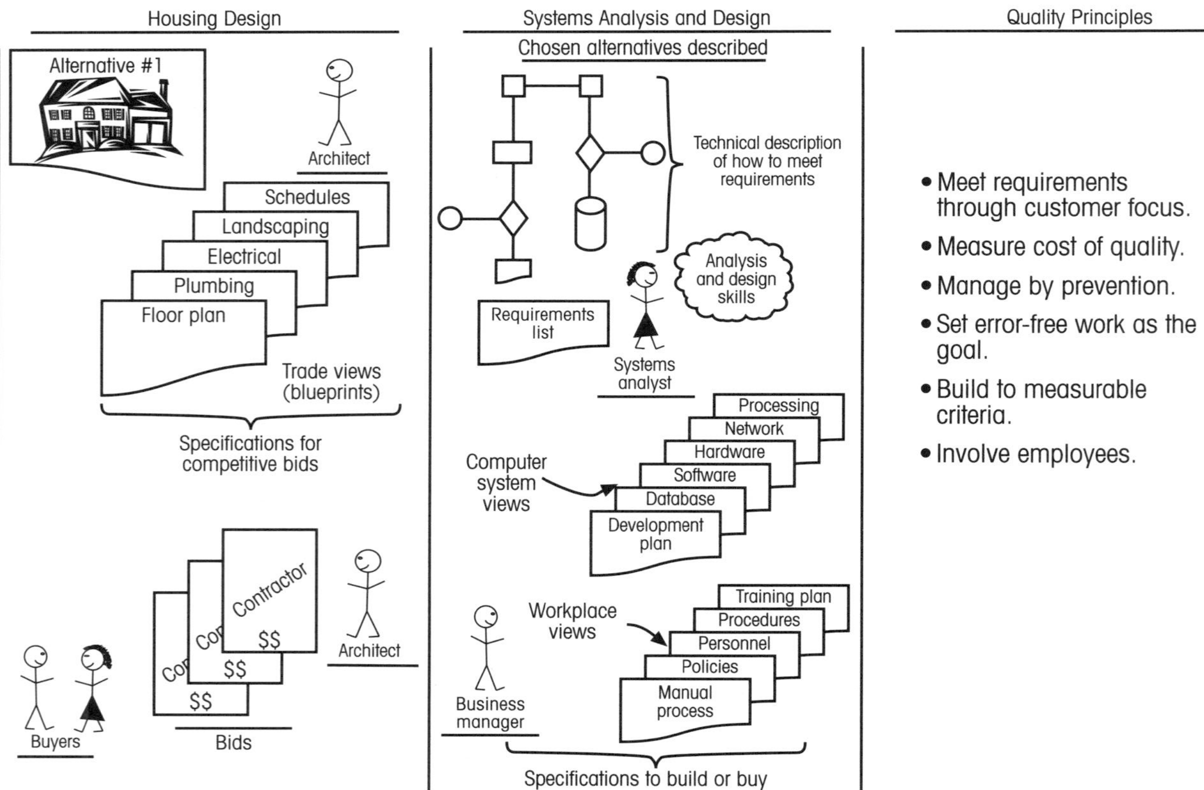

Figure 7.1. Analysis and design.

Housing Design

The development activities of this phase are directed at preparing detailed specifications of the high-level design of the selected alternative. This means translating the design into specific *trade views* that are sufficiently informative to satisfy the following objectives.

- Inform construction crews of the desired finished product of each trade element to be assembled or integrated into the house.
- Provide integration of the various trade views, (there may be as many as 16), so that construction is conducted soundly and efficiently.
- Identify building materials and estimate the costs for those materials. These estimates will be partially influenced by the quality of construction and the accoutrements and appliances desired and financed by the buyers. The question of affordability has previously been resolved during the feasibility stage but should be kept in mind.
- Provide sufficient information for contractors to submit competitive bids for all or part of the work.

The last objective presupposes that the architect and buyers have selection criteria other than just price. Such criteria may include experience, reputation, size and stability of construction companies, and skill levels of individual artisans. It is common during this process to obtain the services of a general contractor who acts as a construction project integrator. This includes overall responsibility for final delivery. The general contractor may assign current employees to the project, hire new laborers, or sublet the work. The general contractor is responsible for generating the final, detailed, working blueprints and instructions to the trade view work crews. Sometimes, the architect may perform this function and provide the blueprints and instructions to the general contractor.

Systems Analysis and Design

An examination of Figure 7.1 reveals the level of IT system design activity required to overcome the poor success rates depicted in Figure 1.2.

This is done by ensuring that the business system incorporates all the elements (automated as well as manual) of the workplace environment.

The design process depicts technical views of the chosen alternative, complemented by the workplace views required for the system to be successful in day-to-day operation. Experience shows that the insertion of technology into the workplace can result in disruptions and service degradations unless manual work process modifications are consciously planned and designed as well.

Computer System Views

Computer system views serve the same purpose for the IT system as trade views serve with the house. Each view describes the specific components of an automated system in enough detail to satisfy the following objectives.

- Construct and integrate, using hardware and software components, a computer processing system that improves, and does not impede, the business' work process. This will likely include a database component and a network element to facilitate communications.
- Construct the system to the required levels of quality and performance demanded of the work process activity.
- Construct the system in a timely fashion while allowing for thoroughness of testing.
- Allow for efficient use of technical and human resources during construction.
- Deliver a system that can be operated, upgraded, and maintained within a reasonably accurate cost projection.

Due to the unforgiving nature of computers, great detail is required in the finished design documents. This is because they act as blueprints to those individuals involved in the system's construction.

As with the housing example, decisions are required whether to develop the system using internal personnel, contract employees, or a combination of both. In all cases, an extremely detailed and accurate degree of documentation must be generated and maintained for several reasons.

System narratives and goal and objective statements serve as the written agreement between business managers and technologists. These constitute a statement of work in a contracting situation.

Documentation of the various computer system views should adhere to national and international standards.* This will minimize ambiguity and guard against becoming locked into a vendor's nonstandard proprietary solution. The implications of this are presented in chapter 3. As discussed, lock-in describes a condition where only the original information service provider can understand what the system does and how it works. Standardization in documentation also guards against confusion on the provider's team should it experience turnover during the project's execution or during the system's operation.

Documentation of the system views provides the basis for selecting equipment components and software packages. It also guides their integration with the business process being supported. These views should include future sizing estimates based on the growth projections of the business process.

Documentation of the data views is especially critical since database integrity is central to any IT project. Corrupted data can literally destroy a business. It is especially insidious since it can happen over a period of time, and it is difficult to identify in its early stages.

Finally, system documentation forms the basis for an enforceable contract and is the starting point for resolving contract disagreements. The bottom line in resolving any contract dispute is the statement of work or the specification stating what was contracted for, what was deemed acceptable by the customer, when it was to be delivered, and at what price.

Comprehensive IT system design documentation should include the following views. They should generally be prepared in the sequence described in the following sections.

---

* Documentation standards for automated system projects are available through ASQC or the National Institute for Science and Technology, U.S. Department of Commerce. A pertinent guideline for use here is ISO 9000-3.

Data View Documentation

Data view documentation outlines, for the developer, exactly what to include: in the database; in standard definitions and codes for data items in order to eliminate ambiguities; and in record and file structure descriptions that result in efficient, effective, and economical storage and retrieval. Security and integrity controls need to be precisely defined in terms of who can access what data and under what circumstances the data can be changed or copied. There is also the question of file backups and the survivability of business records. These must be included in the database design documentation and must be based on the demands of the business process.

Processing View Documentation

Processing view documentation outlines the detailed manipulations of the data by logic formulae in the step-by-step fashion required by the computer for successful execution. This processing logic forms the basis for selecting off-the-shelf software, writing tailored software, selecting hardware, and designing networks. As a minimum, this type of documentation includes work flow diagrams, data entity and relationship charts, high-level programming flowcharts, and narratives. Processing documentation should reflect, in detail, the interfaces with the manual processes and procedures of the workplace as seen in Figure 1.3. These two aspects of the system need to be developed concurrently so they will complement each other.

Processing documentation should also include a clear description of error prevention, detection, and correction processing. Error processing is critical to the maintenance of database integrity, business processing efficiency, and customer problem resolution.

Finally, processing documentation should include how the software and system will be tested during construction. Testing criteria (that is, measures against which software and system success are judged) are identified; test scenarios are developed; and test programs are written.

A Software View Documentation

A software view, or program specification, provides programmers with the level of detail necessary to actually code and create software. These instructions differ according to the program language used. Languages vary according to the type of processing application and other project characteristics. When off-the-shelf software packages are selected, a new degree of complexity and uncertainty, in the name of simplicity and lower cost, enters the picture. Complexity increases as the need to integrate disparate software from differing vendors increases; and uncertainty escalates as the degree of complexity and the number of involved vendors expands.

All of the issues discussed in chapter 4 come to impact the project at this point, and risk factors rise accordingly. Unless open system standards are used as a selection factor, the proprietary uniqueness and incompatibilities among the various software elements can make the system extremely difficult to integrate. Even within standards, many software products have proprietary hooks that make integration of different vendor software packages difficult.

Hardware View Documentation

Hardware views tend to be the easiest to formulate, since physical components that have clear functions to perform are involved. There are computing elements, memory devices, and terminals for performing input and for viewing output. There are also printers and communication elements that link them all together. All of these components work under the control of operating system software. Compatibility and interoperability are the keys to successful hardware integration and utilization.

The hardware view should clearly define the standards against which compatibility and interoperability are measured. These standards are then used to select appropriate equipment. There are two ways to identify such standards: (1) closed proprietary and (2) open systems.

The advantages and disadvantages of open systems were discussed, as were the benefits and liability of staying within a vendor's closed standard. At this time, a decision needs to be made regarding which approach to standards to follow. It should also be stated here that software standards should be given top priority over hardware, unless it is impractical to do so because of an overriding hardware constraint or existing investment in equipment.

Workplace View Documentation

Of equal importance, with the computer system view, is the complementary workplace view describing how the work flow and employee manual activities are modified to integrate smoothly with the automated portion of the business process. Experience indicates that few attempts at automation have given this area the attention it requires. During the alternatives analysis phase, proposed system solutions were examined for operational, as well as for technical and economic feasibility. In fact, the overriding factor should have been operational. A judgment was made as to which proposed solution best fit with the existing workplace's environment. This is created by policies and personnel practices, position descriptions, instructions, procedures, and the manual processes currently employed in the conduct of business and when dealing with customers.

When technology systems have been rated fully successful, it is because the system has improved the effectiveness and efficiency of employees in the workplace and with the business' customers. Even marginally successful systems have been credited with contributing some positive aspect to the overall business process. But, those failed efforts have been judged to actually detract from successful prosecution of the business. These systems are often judged to be impediments to the successful execution of employee job functions: They actually make it harder for employees to do their duties and satisfy their customers. This has been the case, because time and again, a technical system is thrust upon unprepared workers, and their manual procedures and instruction have not reflected the changes necessitated by the technology system.

The purpose of the operational feasibility analysis was to determine this degree of change and factor it into the proposed alternatives decision process. Having consciously evaluated workplace changes, these must be made to the workplace procedures concurrent with the design of the technology support system.

These changes usually require more than just the training needed to operate the technical facets of the new system. At a minimum, the following workplace views should be carefully reviewed and modified—if necessary—to reflect the changes that automation is making on task and job execution.

- Personnel policies
- Position descriptions
- Manual procedures
- Management oversight functions
- Employees' aptitudes for certain tasks
- Employee evaluation criteria
- Job (work) flows
- Problem resolution procedures (trouble desk)
- Documentation and instructions
- Training plans and materials
- Auditing procedures

It should be noted that all eventual modifications will not be known at the same time, so this issue needs to be revisited periodically. Besides that, changes in the business, after system installation, will occur, and these will further affect workplace-related views.

No matter how complete the job of requirements definition, changes over the life of the system will occur. It is important to test these changes on a small scale before wholesale introduction to the business work process. A commonly used technique for accomplishing this testing is to pilot the changes at a stable work location, running them in parallel with the existing way of doing business. The benefits of a pilot is that bugs and other unanticipated problems are discovered and corrected before the change is implemented companywide. While it may seem expensive and perhaps unnecessary, it is an effective risk-reduction strategy, and it helps ensure continued quality service to the vast majority of customers.

Conducting pilot and parallel operations contributes greatly to the understanding of how the system will impact the workplace. Through actual execution of the technical aspects of the system, the workplace can be fine-tuned after interfacing with some real-world customers.

Specifications to Build or Buy

In preparing for system construction, all computer system and workplace views must be sufficiently documented to direct the activities of contractors and/or in-house development staff. In preparing this documentation, the architect/analyst will probably seek the assistance of specialists in the hardware, software, network, and database approach associated with the chosen alternative. The overall controlling document prepared at this time is the development plan. This is done by the analyst in coordination with the business managers overseeing the workplace modifications.

If the technical specifications are used in soliciting contractor assistance in system construction, then they must be definitive and firm enough to allow contractors to prepare bids. These specifications must also be definitive and firm enough to select, and perhaps defend, a decision to go with one contractor over another. This may include being able to justify a decision to higher authorities when the selected contractor did not submit the lowest price. Justifying other than lowest price requires a clear and concise statement of requirements and the ability to show greater overall value to the company.

The more business managers can relate the selected contractor's technical proposal to a well-thought-out workplace implementation and be able to show how the contractor's solution will integrate into the workplace without experiencing disruptions or dissatisfied customers, the easier the internal sale will be. The architect/analyst can assist in formulating these specifications—the criteria by which contractors will be evaluated—and can help in selling or defending the evaluation to higher authorities. The ability to view the long-term advantages of one contractor's proposal over another comes with experience, knowing the issues affecting the industry, and knowing the questions to ask about the bidders' proposals. This may indeed be the situation where the architect/analyst's objectivity reaps the biggest dividends.

Contracting for the System

A few books are concerned with the proper way to contract various elements of computer support. And since disputes are increasingly common in this arena, there will be no shortage of reading material in the years ahead. Be sure to seek advice from a lawyer with experience in contracting for automated data processing support and one who is practicing in the field. But even knowledgeable and practicing lawyers may not fully appreciate the kinds and/or degree of damage that may be inflicted on a business through failures attributed to an IT system. Of special concern to business managers are the following types of failures and their impacts on the business. To the greatest extent possible, a business wants access to legal advice and contracting language that can protect it against the following:

- Damages resulting from project overruns and nondelivery
- Escalating expenses due to continual expansion of a system that was not competently sized to meet the business requirement
- Downtime considered excessive when compared to similar types of systems in similar businesses environments
- Damages to customers or internal business activities due to inaccurate customer or business information resulting from hardware, database, or software failures that should have been anticipated, prevented, or for which error detection and recovery routines would have reduced damage
- Damages resulting from the compromise of company-sensitive data or from violations of the confidentiality of customer records
- Expenses associated with the recovery of lost information due to hardware, database, software, or communications failure
- Lost revenues due to system outages
- Revenue losses due to corporate reputation damage brought on by poor system performance

Note that even though various loss incidents can be addressed in the contract, additional protection against business loss should be met with insurance.

Many of these categories of loss are not within the usual experience of business managers and need to be given some thought. There is a ripple effect that, upon reflection, can be identified with most computers uses. For example, the use of erroneous data can adversely affect an endless number of transactions, decisions, and customers before the error is discovered and corrected. In some cases, restitution may be necessary for damages incurred by customers during this period.

To provide focus to these issues of loss and potential damage, one of the contemporary tools available is the technique of risk management. In simple terms, risk management allows business managers to systematically identify the value of all assets associated with the system, giving special attention to the intangible or soft assets such as information, customer service, and company reputation. Next, weaknesses in the processing environment (manual as well as automated) are identified, and a probability factor is assigned to their occurrence. A potential loss per occurrence is then estimated with a politically acceptable weight assigned.

To this point, a risk management analysis has produced a priority list of undesirable events or actions that result in some estimated loss to the business. Used in this way, risk management can assist business managers in the following ways.

- The ripple effect of the system is explored, with the obvious as well as the extended uses of system outputs being identified.
- Overall system value is often enhanced through the identification of extended users and uses.
- Possible causes of system disruptions and contamination can be identified; potential losses can be estimated; and protective and recovery strategies can become part of the design.
- This knowledge is essential for proposing adequate contracting protections and serves as a foundation for other legal actions if required.

Thus, risk management is one of the most powerful tools available to business managers in their quest for quality and performance in systems.

Quality Principles Employed

QM principles can greatly influence the efforts to design a successful system. It is during design that the definition of quality and its attributes—identified and specified during requirements definition—are satisfied in the system construction views. These guide the development efforts of the next phase. It is imperative that they reflect how quality is specified in the actual instructions followed by analysts, programmers, testers, and others during programming and integration. Typically, the how of quality is expressed in the following:

- Design documents governing collection of source data
- Edit routines that screen erroneous data at the source
- Error detection and correction routines
- Database management and integrity controls
- Validation and verification checkpoints where the accuracy of program logic and algorithms are assessed
- Checkpoints where fraud and abusive system manipulation are detected
- Logs where required audit trails are generated
- Controls on outputs to ensure secure and confidential delivery of information products

All of these quality-oriented processing activities are incorporated into the step-by-step execution of the business system as expressed in both the technical and manual portions of the process.

It is the business managers' responsibility to review these quality-oriented processing steps for adequacy. Concurrently, it is the architect/analyst's responsibility to ensure that these steps are properly expressed, as specifications, in each of the views that guide system construction.

Additionally, there are certain system stability issues that need to be addressed if the IT system is to function reliably. These include the following:

- Placement of computer equipment in the properly conditioned environments
- Existence of systems documentation sufficient to diagnose problems and take corrective action
- Training and cross-training adequate for employees and/or contract support personnel to accomplish their assigned duties in a timely fashion
- Documented and exercised emergency backup and recovery procedures
- Policies and procedures governing how changes are made in the processing environment so that quality service is maintained

The process of meeting requirements during development requires the continual reinforcement of quality principles. First and foremost, never lose focus on the customer. You have gone to great lengths to identify and agree on the business process requirements, the quality attributes, and the technical and manual processing support requirements. Requirements have been validated during the early development phases in order to be satisfied during the design and construction phases.

Success criteria for the systems project need to be identified in measurable business terms or against some established standard of acceptable performance. Having been established, measures and standards must now be used throughout the rest of development to monitor progress and judge whether quality is being built into the system.

Meeting quality and performance requirements is best accomplished through a design that promotes the error-free execution of the work process each time, every time. The primary output from the design phase is the specification of an error-free work process for use in the workplace. During the design phase, preventive thinking should be liberally practiced. Different business disciplines and expertises, such as security, operations management, and audit, need to participate if preventive thinking is going to be effective and productive. The practice of preventive thinking is an attempt to prove Murphy wrong—not everything that can go wrong need go wrong! Preventive thinking requires knowledge and imagination, and should be performed throughout the early stages of the project in order to anticipate problems that could jeopardize success.

Each of the conditions discussed in chapter 4 needs to be periodically revisited for possible negative impact on both the technical and the managerial aspects of the project. Preventive thinking reduces problems that can cause waste, scrap, rework, and expensive late development phase corrections. This cost-of-quality sensitivity allows the developer to deliver a high-quality system by correcting errors, flaws, misunderstandings, and omissions during the low-cost definition and design phases while the system is still malleable. Cost overruns are less likely to occur when preventive thinking is central to the design phase.

None of the principles can be effective without the good-faith involvement of employees who have been empowered to practice quality thinking. Such involvement is the result of teamwork between the nontechnical managers' employees and the technical staff constructing the automated system aspects. This teamwork flourishes only if it is patterned after the cooperation demonstrated by the senior managers responsible for project success. Leadership is required!

Summary

The SDP activities to this point have concentrated on definition, analysis, and design. In the language of quality, these activities are essential to doing right things (DRT). The remaining chapters deal with constructing the system right the first time (RFT). The preparation may be great—but can you follow through?

CHAPTER 8

Automating the Business Requirement (Part 4): Construction and Integration Phase

House Construction

Up to this point, all activities have had but one goal, the cost-efficient and quality construction of the house. Even with clear and concise trade views, the task of construction calls for close supervision to ensure the quality of the final dwelling and its acceptance by the buyers and other involved parties. These include building inspectors and warrantors.

It is the construction contractor's responsibility to provide guidance, supervision, and project management to complete the house on time and within budget. The contractor's time and cost estimates were based on the architect's specifications (that is the views) and other information provided at the conclusion of the design phase. The winning construction contractor must now schedule work tasks and coordinate the arrival of building materials. Employees or subcontractors must do the work according to a sequence and in the shortest possible time frame.

As Figure 8.1 indicates, there are a great many activities to keep in order, and many problems could arise. This will test the contractor's management skills. Using the language of quality, the first four phases of the development process have dealt with *doing the right thing*; that is, meeting the customer's requirement. But no matter how accurate, clear, and concise the specifications, the finished house can be less than quality due to faulty construction practices and poor contractor management. During

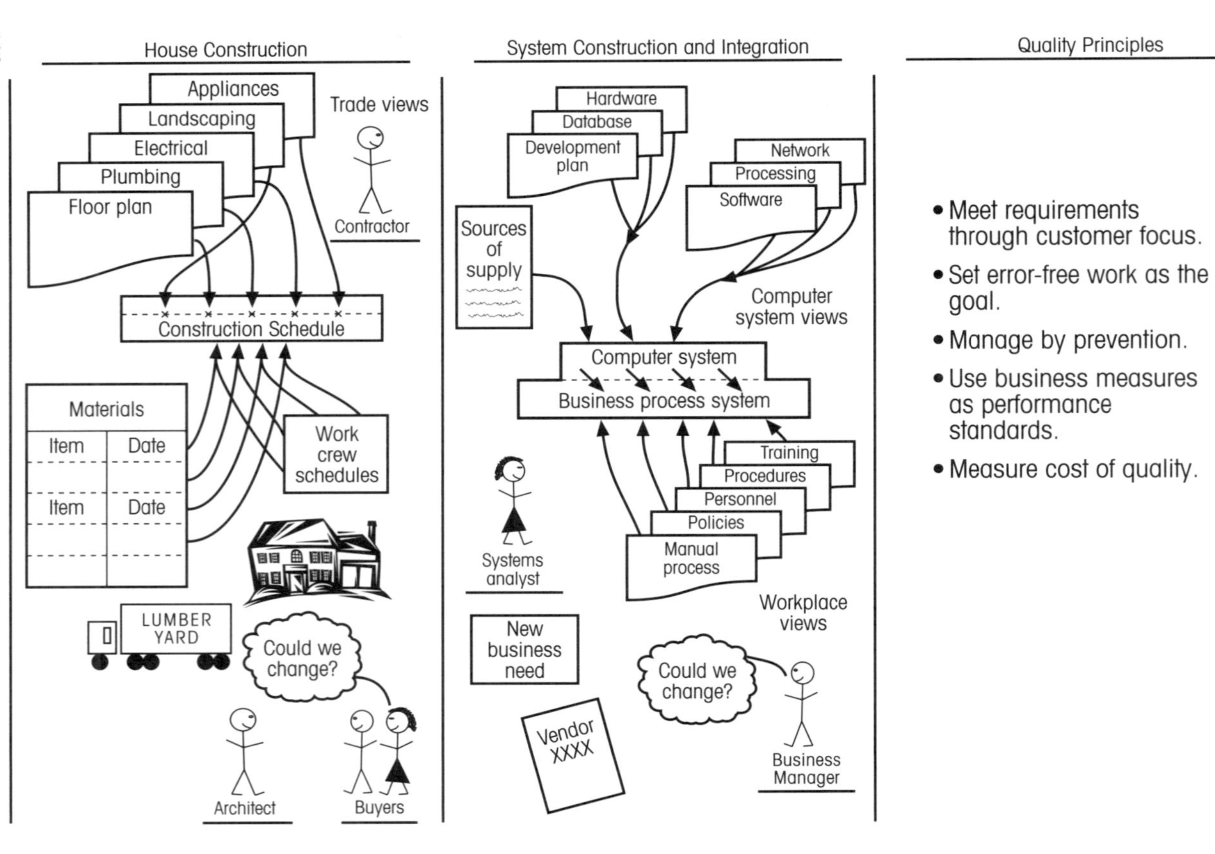

Figure 8.1. Construction and integration.

this phase of development, the contractor must be concerned with *doing things right the first time*; that is, performing the actual steps of construction according to sound building practices and with skilled and supervised labor.

The contractor's management skills are similar to those exercised by managers of any complex undertaking. The traditional functions of management and supervision apply to the following:

- Planning and budgeting
- Staffing and organizing
- Directing and coordinating
- Controlling and monitoring

While the views provide construction guidance, and the materials list identifies what to order; it is the scheduling of construction work activities that brings the house to reality. The schedule must be accomplished within a finite amount of time expressed in the budget. Work materials are delivered in a sequence determined by the schedule. Work crews of proper expertise are employed at the site on arrival of the appropriate materials. Plumbers do not stand around waiting for the foundation to dry. Roofers do not charge time to the project until the frame is up.

Work crews should be competent and employed in enough numbers to allow for efficient, smooth construction. They should not be so few that activity lags or so plentiful that they get in each other's way.

The contractor is responsible for staffing the construction project with competent laborers and technicians and organizing their efforts according to work schedules. These provide the script for directing and coordinating the effort of all employees and subcontractors and the delivery of construction materials.

Once begun, construction activities must be closely monitored and controlled. This is accomplished by continually referring to the views and the construction plans to compare what is being built against what was designed.

The challenge of *right the first time* is answered by comparing actual construction work against good practices of the building industry and against the prevailing building codes. Monitoring and controlling the construction effort is only as effective as the contractor and the level of external review from code inspectors. Because of this, the architect may perform an additional function of obtaining independent opinions concerning construction soundness. Such appraisals, while adding to cost, can be justified by discovering flaws in construction early enough to allow correction at the lowest possible cost. Thus, this prevents budget overruns.

Ascertaining a level of quality is a judgment comprised by determining adherence to construction codes (minimum) plus additional steps taken during construction to deliver a stable and easily maintained house. Additionally, certain high-quality accoutrements may have been specified for installation. The presence of such features satisfy customer desires and add overall value to the dwelling.

Effective management of the construction process should identify problems early so as to allow timely and low-cost correction. If flaws are not discovered until final inspection, or even after delivery, the correction costs can be astronomical. Supervision and continuous checks on quality can prevent the vast majority of costly, late construction corrective actions.

Late construction corrections brought about by a change in requirements or desires is another matter. Changes during construction can be costly; they can even jeopardize the building's integrity. Cosmetic changes may merely increase the final cost; but desiring a picture window in the middle of a load-bearing wall may force significant modifications to the overall construction plan that result in a ripple of fixes throughout the whole building.

The previous phases of development concentrated on meeting requirements, and it is against those requirements that all construction plans and estimates were made. Changes during construction should be minimized and limited to the cosmetic, or else major cost overruns and schedule delays may result.

System Construction and Integration

The analogy of house construction has been helpful to this point, but a new level of complexity now enters the scene: That is, home buyers do not generally have to live in the house while it is being constructed. But the automation of a business process does not take place in a laboratory apart from the real world of employees and customers. In fact, the principles of QM urge extensive participation by all involved parties during the development phases, in order to define and validate requirements and to verify that construction of the system is following sound and accepted practices. To do this, there has to be an interplay between the new technical aspects of the business process and the old or current way of executing the process. Unless the new is totally new the interplay becomes vital for determining operational readiness and deciding when to introduce the technology into the work place. With this as background, the discussion in chapter 7 concerning pilot/parallel strategies takes on added meaning.

System construction and integration may well have to be staged in phases so that technical problems and risks to the business are reduced. With system projects, it is common to implement certain technical aspects, test them out during a pilot/parallel operation, and then integrate the remaining aspects until the whole system is operational. Commonly, database creation is a first step since file conversions take time due to data validation and data cleanup chores.

Successive steps often deal with source data collection and edit processes. These can be programmed and implemented as stand-alone elements of the entire system. They can be thoroughly tested and integrated with the appropriate workplace procedure before companywide implementation. Report generation and data retrieval routines can also be implemented as subsystems of the whole. Finally, network subsystems can be brought on-line in a controlled and evolutionary fashion that limit risk.

Figure 8.1 illustrates this integration of workplace views with those specifying the functional parts of the supporting computer system. As in the case of house construction, a project manager is required to coordinate all actions of this phase and to ensure that elements of the IT system are consistent with the modified policies, procedures, and manual processes of the workplace.

Key among required documents is the development plan, which outlines the sequence of actions needed to assemble and test stand-alone system elements. It also describes the interrelationships among the various system elements as prescribed by the design.

From a project management perspective, the challenge is to manage the effort according to plan and not let the more-interesting technical activities surge ahead of the less-glamorous administrative tasks or the workplace procedural modifications. This calls for careful scheduling of independent development tasks and integration of the whole.

If the analytic tasks of the previous phases have been accomplished, and if the effort has been guided by quality principles, then there can be a high degree of confidence in the technical approach being implemented. Each of the previous phases have focused on doing the right things, reducing risk by deliberately performing tests of feasibility, and asking the what-if questions prompted by preventive thinking.

Again, as with the house construction, business managers must be concerned with the soundness of system construction activities as they are being carried out by the development team. Is the team following prescribed and professionally recognized methods in the actual programming, testing, integration, and assembly of the system? From the managers' perspective, how can the soundness of system construction and integration activities be determined?

Project Management Activities

First, do the in-house or contract employees appear to be adequately supervised? Is the effort being managed? The project manager's skill requirements are the same as those of the general contractor. They are

- Planning and budgeting
- Staffing and organizing
- Directing and coordinating
- Controlling and monitoring

During the systems construction and integration phase, all of these functions must be performed not only by the IT project leader but also by the business managers responsible for workplace modifications.

The project leader and business managers must plan and budget for the utilization of technical systems personnel and representative workplace employees. They must be available for consultation and to conduct tests on the system as it is integrated into the workplace's operating procedures.

A common challenge to project success is often the failure to properly staff and organize the system construction and integration phase. If the technical design being implemented was the result of a least-risk approach to solving the business' problems, the staffing issue should pose no serious problem, since the marketplace can usually provide a reasonable supply of people possessing the required skills. On the other hand, a pioneering design or a determination to use emerging, and therefore high-risk technologies, may meet with severe and very expensive staffing problems due to a scarcity of qualified technicians. Continuity and backup are also personnel issues that become manageable if the project uses tried-and-trusted technologies. But continuity and backup can become a nightmare if the one and only expert on the team decides to leave, and no replacement can be found.

In recent years, the importance of formal education for systems personnel has been recognized. This is especially true for systems analysts involved in the definition and design phases of development and for the management and supervision of the construction phase. The mere presence of degreed personnel, however, cannot guarantee that a quality system will be delivered when the project itself is mismanaged. If requirements are unclear, if customer expectations are unreal, if resource and budget estimates are inaccurate, and if time frames for delivery are overly optimistic, then all the Ph.D.'s in the world will not be able to deliver a quality system *and* satisfy the customers' business requirements. Either there will be cost overruns and schedule delays, or construction quality will suffer as shortcuts are taken to keep on schedule and within budget.

While it may be comforting to know that formally educated personnel are working on your system, remember that comprehensiveness and competency of project management are better indicators of success or failure.

Business managers have different staffing and organizational concerns. During the early phases of systems development, it is usually quite easy to obtain participants from the appropriate business process area. The idea of using technology to support a new way of doing business is either exciting or threatening. In either case, the turnout for initial project meetings is high, and participation is good. If the project endeavors to reengineer a work process, commonly employed facilitation techniques usually promote a great deal of involvement as business process representatives first reach consensus on how things are currently done and then reach agreement on what the reengineered process should look like and how it will function. But as time passes and technicians and managers are doing the more mundane tasks, some interest is likely lost. Throw in a couple of delays due to budget or acquisition problems, and team continuity can become an issue. As this occurs, business managers must take measures to ensure that adequate (that is, skills, levels, and knowledge) worker representation continues to be involved in the development effort, especially during the construction and integration phase. With new employees' inevitable involvement, business managers must closely monitor the insertion of new ideas and requirements that may have been previously considered and discarded. While new team representatives may indeed have legitimate ideas, project completion could be placed in jeopardy by making changes to requirements or design. Such new ideas and requirements must be examined at senior management levels when deciding the fate of the suggested changes.

A legitimate change to system requirements, and to subsequent design documents, needs to be carefully examined. An impact analysis should be conducted to determine whether the benefit gained by the change offsets the difficulties, risk, and added expense of implementation. Figure 8.2, a variation of Figure 3.2, illustrates the relative cost to fix an error or omission at various phases of the SDP. Of course, true changing business requirements have to be accommodated with both the technical and

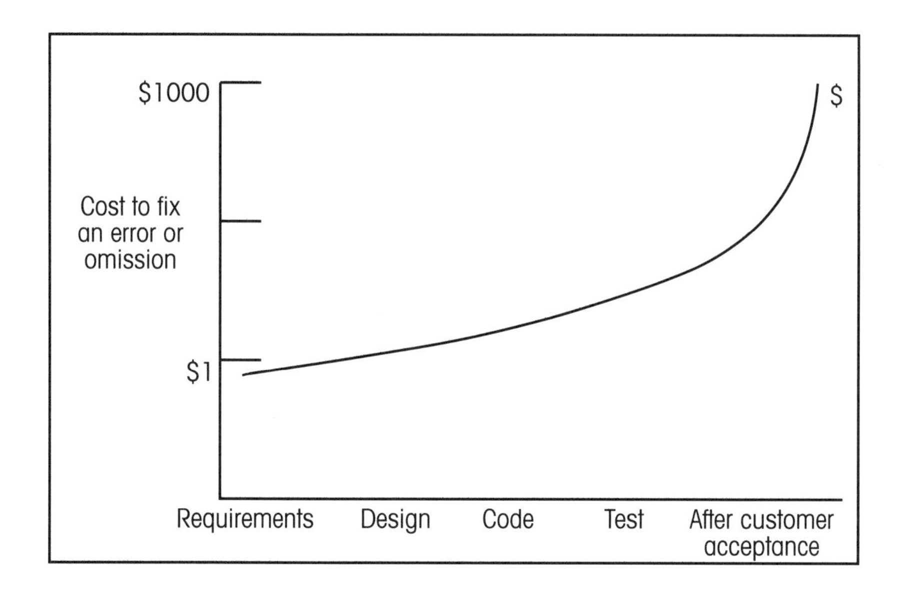

Figure 8.2. Relative cost to fix an error or omission in an IT project.

workplace systems being adjusted accordingly. Otherwise, IT becomes a force constraining the business. It is just that changes during construction and integration can be very disruptive and expensive, and they should not be entered into frivolously.

Directing and coordinating are also key to successful construction. Purchase of hardware and software components must be coordinated with the availability of technical personnel. Work spaces and computer rooms must be prepared and ready to receive equipment. Contrary to popular belief, not everything required for an automated system can fit under a desk or on it. File servers, printers, and communications equipment should still be secured in environmentally conditioned rooms with adequate backup power.

Project managers should be using control tools and techniques on even the smallest projects. These techniques go by various names and acronyms: program evaluation and review technique (PERT) and critical path method (CPM) are two such techniques. They are used to keep track of resources and to evaluate progress and resource usage against the planned sequence of tasks. Pathways of task execution, critical to timely completion of the construction, are identified for special observation. Deviations from a critical path, in either elapsed time or resource usage, indicate that the total effort is ahead of or behind schedule. The project will be at or near budget, or it will be over budget. The use of such techniques signify an attempt at professional project management.

The use of such techniques make possible the realistic day-to-day monitoring and controlling of the project's progress and the efficient use of available resources. If one set of tasks is behind schedule while another is ahead, it may be possible to redirect resources from the completed area of work to the area experiencing difficulty. This level of management attention ensures that highly priced technical personnel are not sitting idly by while other project areas get further behind. The only major proviso deals with whether the available technical resource persons possess the required knowledge and skills to actually contribute and not merely get in the way.

Through all of this, nontechnical business managers and the architect/analyst must remain involved with the technical effort and must closely monitor progress against the development plan. Progress reviews should be conducted often enough to obtain a feel for developing problems and to assess their impact on other scheduled events. Some problems may indicate flaws in the design or in the quality of hardware and software support systems originating from external suppliers. Problems of this kind may require that the system design be revisited. The design may have to be adjusted to realities that were not apparent or that did not exist during the design phase. The earlier such problems are discovered, the easier they will be to correct. Again, the reality of Figure 8.2 must be taken into account for the impact that changes and problems will have on both budget and schedule.

Management Activities: A Frame of Mind

It may or may not be true that a graduate of the minute manager institute could successfully direct a *Fortune* 500 company or that an MBA is indeed better suited for the job. What is a fact, is that all types and kinds of managers, regardless of education, have experienced frustration with IT projects.

Much has been written over the years of the creativity needed to work with computers and how experimentation is required to devise truly elegant solutions. Generally, a solution is judged to be elegant by other computer personnel and can lead to overly complex and impressive (at least to other computer people) systems. The problem is that a systems solution of an overly creative kind is often overkill, full of bugs, difficult to maintain, and difficult to use. No doubt creativity and inventiveness have a place in the development of some systems, but they should be kept in close check during development of *your* business process support systems. The entire approach taken by this book is to reduce risk to the business while improving process efficiency and effectiveness. Project management of the construction phase must also proceed from a *least-risk* perspective. The easiest way to achieve this is through preventive thinking. The ability to anticipate problems and think in terms of operational impacts is a prerequisite for project management. The many variants of Murphy's Law may seem a joke to most people but not to a project manager. Some think the best preparation for a project manager of an automation effort is to raise children. Business managers, too, need to practice a healthy degree of caution and at times be skeptical. Creativity and inventiveness must be constructively directed through experienced management. This means that all of the management functions are taken seriously by the project manager and not glossed over in discussions. Business managers should also perceive a mature sense of responsibility on the part of the IT project manager. These attitudes are essential for maintaining a proper frame of mind regarding management of any automation effort.

Validation, Verification, and Test

Another activity that must be observed by business managers during system construction and integration is the regular practice of validation, verification, and test (VV&T). For purposes of this book, these functions are synonymous with quality assurance and embody the principles of QM. Validation has previously been practiced during both the definition and design phase to assure all parties were doing the right thing. Concurrence by the users, management, auditors, security personnel, and others was actively sought to validate their collective requirements for the system and to confirm that the design did, in fact, meet these requirements. During the construction and integration phase, requirements and designs must be revalidated to ensure that actual system components and software elements are not integrated in a way that ignores or negates an established business need. This ability to trace requirements through the construction phase of the system is essential to final acceptance of the system by business managers.

Verification and testing deal with the examination of system development work products and help to ascertain whether

- Hardware and software components have been programmed and integrated properly.
- System components deliver the required results—expected of the design—to satisfy the business requirement.

The principal way to determine soundness of development is to observe a close correlation between actual project execution and the concepts set forth in this book. (Other books on systems analysis and design or project management for systems development may also be helpful.) The architect/analyst can also perform an independent assessment for the thoroughness and completeness of development actions conducted by the in-house or contract developer. Another way to get a handle on the issue of soundness is determined by system tests and a thorough review of testing documentation.

The extent of a VV&T effort must be determined by the criticality of the business process being supported. How VV&T is performed is also dictated by the criticality of the application's function. For a parking lot permit system, perhaps the VV&T actions of the programmer can be considered adequate. For a financial management support system, perhaps a peer review of a team of independent developers from within the company will suffice. But, for an air traffic control application, nothing but a completely independent review by external testing groups could be considered sufficient.

The adequacy of VV&T activities can also become a decisive factor in the arbitration of any liability claim. This may be against your business, should a customer experience system-related loss, and in the subsequent action you would bring against your contract developer or components supplier.

Historically, system testing activities have been given little attention until the final delivery and acceptance phase of the project. But, to be truly effective, testing must be an ongoing activity during the process of definition, design, and construction. To wait until the system is delivered is to guarantee the unacceptability of many of its facets and to incur the costs depicted by Figures 3.2 and 8.2. Generally, business managers should find evidence of the following:

- A test effort separate from the development effort
- Plans outlining what aspects of the system, both automated and manual, are to be tested
- Existence of criteria against which testing results are compared (that is, the measures of quality attributes that were defined during the requirements phase)
- Testing budget and schedule
- Test packages with documentation describing the tests and how they are to be performed—this should be in enough detail that a systems professional, other than the original tester, could execute the tests at a later time
- Test recommendations

Phased Implementation

In chapter 7, the practice of system implementation by way of a pilot and/or parallel operation was discussed. The reason for this design strategy was to reduce risk to the business process when a technology system was inserted. Popular in the jargon of technologists is the term *turnkey.* The implication of a turnkey has always been the ease with which a system can be activated. Turnkey implementations, however, can subject a business to an inordinately high degree of risk while a safer course is the pilot/parallel operation approach. When conducting a pilot/parallel implementation, the system is first tried out in a stable, real-world, yet low-risk setting. Usually a medium sized or volume business unit is ideal so that employees have time to accustom themselves to the new way of doing business. Also, organizations should never check the system out with only their best and brightest people. This proves nothing!

A crosscut of all employees expected to use the system should be selected to staff the pilot tests. The training they receive should be the same as that planned for all other employees. To protect against system failures or operator errors, the pilot should be run in parallel with the current method of carrying out the business activity. While this will impose an additional short-term workload, the need to guarantee correctness and successful completion of the transaction, while maintaining good customer relations, demands it.

Documentation Completeness

Perhaps the most effective way to judge the soundness of a systems development effort is through the quality of the documentation generated and assembled. Documentation is the most universally ignored aspect of a systems development effort next only to testing. This is because document preparation is dull and boring work while analysis, design, programming, and integration are exciting. Documenting what has been done and what is being done is tedious, and besides, it is always assumed that the programmer knows how the system works. Isn't that enough? This last rationale for incomplete and poorly compiled documentation is a special threat when the systems effort has been an in-house undertaking. It is far too easy for user and technical staff familiarity and ease of communication to substitute for the written word. This invariably leads to a critical dependence on key technical staffers and all the associated risks that such a dependence brings. At least a contractor-developed system documentation can be treated as a deliverable item requiring acceptance before payments are made. It is usually difficult to get documentation to an acceptable degree of completion with an in-house effort since it is viewed as a by-product. Thus, the attitude, "we can always do it later."

What constitutes acceptable and usable documentation? To a great extent, this is determined by the operational and maintenance philosophy for the system; namely, whether operations and maintenance will be an in-house responsibility or done under contract. From a documentation standpoint, the initial reaction of most people is to view the in-house operations requirement as being more stringent than that completed by the contractor. After all, once the warranties expire, an organization is on its own, and its technical staff must be able to respond to problems and make necessary changes to the system. It is clear in this case that the quality of documentation is essential for continued system maintenance.

It is because an in-house commitment is so obviously complex, critical, and serious that outsourcing has its appeal. Combined with the perceived sense of protection a contract brings to system support arrangements, documentation can easily be viewed as a contractor's responsibility and, therefore, nothing to worry about. Standard contracts, however, usually fall far short of providing adequate compensation, through penalty clauses, for system failure, and downtime. Rapid recovery time, following a failure, is essential for keeping downtime to a minimum and the system running productively. Rapid recovery is directly dependent on the adequacy of systems documentation. Without complete, accurate, and timely documentation, system failures cannot be traced, diagnosed, analyzed, corrected, and tested. Without adequate documentation, the business system stays down, and revenue and customers are lost. Penalty clause amounts cannot begin to make up for these kinds of losses. Yet under an outsource arrangement the organization may have difficulty assessing the condition of the documentation a contractor is using to operate and maintain the system. The business must hope for the best, knowing that any extended downtime can be severely damaging.

A partial solution to this dilemma is to steer away from standard contract language and negotiate penalty clauses—as severe as possible. The very act of negotiation may, in fact, give indicators of the level of confidence the contractor has in the quality of, not only their documentation, but also their systems. Within reason, this tactic will work. Get too demanding, however, and the contractor may agree to anything to get or keep the contract, and then both the business and the contractor will be hoping for the best.

Since documentation can be thought of as the glue holding a system together, what should business managers expect to get? Each phase of development has work products, and each product should be documented to the extent needed so that it is understood by a reasonably skilled independent analyst. For example, Table 8.1 lists the output documents from each development phase discussed thus far.

Finalized documentation at project completion, should include the following:

- Finalized views of both manual system and technical work processes to include narratives and high-level, detailed work and information flowcharts

Table 8.1. Documentation by phase.

Phase	**Documents**
Requirements definition	• Approved statement of requirements • Description of current business process (as it looks today) • Preliminary budget and time estimates
Alternatives analysis	• High-level proposals for meeting the requirements • Feasibility analysis of proposals, including costs and benefits
Systems analysis and design	• Recommended alternatives • Detailed computer systems documentation (to-build views) • Detailed workplace documentation (to-build views) • Specifications to solicit contractor proposals • Criteria for contractor evaluation
Construction and integration	• Computer system documentation (as-built views) • Workplace documentation (as-built views)

- Data and database descriptions; software programs that edit, update, manipulate, and query the database; programs that generate reports; and instructions for properly backing up and securing data
- Operating instructions for system users, technical maintenance personnel, security and audit personnel, and network administrators
- Configuration information for both software and hardware sufficient to perform system maintenance and to make enhancements
- Curriculum and instructional materials sufficient to prepare future employees for system operation and to supplement on-the-job training
- Warranty and maintenance agreements identifying the periods of service and response times expected from the maintenance contractor

Quality Principles Employed

During this phase of system construction and integration, the application of quality principles has started to demonstrate very visible results. Early QM actions taken within each development phase can now be justified as an effective system begins to take shape.

Customer, business, and employee requirements can be met because they have been defined, agreed to, and used to design the systems construction now taking place.

The guiding principle of error-free work has had two related influences on the systems construction phase. First, the automated system is designed to integrate smoothly into the workplace and to help, not hinder, the performance of error-free business activities. Second, to accomplish this, systems construction must adhere to sound development practices and techniques. Project management must formally exercise all traditional management functions, which, in turn, will ensure that proper development practices are indeed followed.

Preventive thinking has enabled the construction phase to proceed on schedule and within budget. Proper planning and pursuit of a least-risk strategy has reduced the unnecessary surprises that often accompany the use of new and unproven technologies. To be sure, some will question this conservative approach to technology, but then, it is not their business that is at risk!

Quality principles have enabled the true cost of quality to be understood and used to evaluate the effectiveness of approaches taken to construct the system. It is now clear that the validation, verification, and test activities of this and previous phases are paying big dividends. Problems discovered during construction are small and mostly cosmetic. They are not of the budget-busting category and will not unduly delay system delivery. If large problems do appear, it is because of valid changes in business direction, and not because sound system development practices were not followed.

The use of measures and standards and their importance to systems construction fall into two categories. First, there are those measures arrived at during requirements definition that reflect the processing and quality attributes demanded of the finished system. Second, there are the industry, national, and international guidelines and practices that should be followed during system construction. These represent the hardware and software language standards that were decided on during the feasibility phase and the sound system construction practices adhered to during programming and systems integration.

Summary

The concentration of effort during the construction and integration phase has been to do things right the first time (RFT). This activity of systems construction requires adherence to the tried and trusted system development practices taught at the university and the execution of traditional management functions to control the effort and deliver value and quality according to plan.

CHAPTER 9

Automating the Business Requirement (Part 5): Inspection and Approval Phase

Delivery and Acceptance

This final phase in the development process covers the essentials of inspections and approvals before delivery of the house or system. This is the big moment when expectations are met and contracts are fulfilled—or they are not!

House Delivery and Walk-Through

All those who have an interest in the quality of the completed structure are active in this final phase. Most visible are the buyers for whom the house was constructed. Their major concern is to take delivery of a dwelling that meets their statement of needs and desires. The architect has this same concern and often accompanies the buyers during their walk-through inspections.

Contractors are anxious for a successful inspection in order to close out obligations and to solidify profits realized from the project. Defects in construction can only harm the contractor as profits shrink, time delays are experienced, and reputations become subject to damage.

Contractor profits may be reduced when defects are discovered that are the contractor's clear responsibility to correct. Time delays in house acceptance can adversely affect not only contractor's profits on this project but also the schedules and profits of other projects while resources are diverted for corrective actions. If such defects are either deviations from the agreed-on specifications or the result of shoddy workmanship, the contractor will generally assume any additional corrective cost out of its profit.

Of course, changes in the buyers' requirements mean a change in project scope, and additional monies from the buyers are sought. As Figure 9.1 illustrates, there are several other parties involved in final acceptance. Included are the building inspector, who is legally responsible to ensure construction code compliance; the warranter, who ensures and guarantees construction integrity for some period of time; and the bankrolling financial institution, which is the *real* owner of the house. All these representatives exercise their special knowledge to protect the buyers' interests and those of others who have a financial or legal stake in the finished house. This protection provides high motivation for a strong quality assurance function during construction, to lessen the reliance on final inspection with its resultant high costs to correct flaws.

System Delivery and Acceptance

If the previous development phases have been conscientiously followed, and if quality principles have been employed, systems delivery and acceptance should go smoothly, and all parties to system construction will feel satisfied and proud of the effort. No major problems are discovered, and the system, as well as workplace modifications, are ready for operation. All deliverables are prepared and in their final form. Hardware, if required, is installed and is functioning to the standard of reliability required of the business process. A mere demonstration of equipment readiness was not considered sufficient, and the newly developed system has been thoroughly tested and run in parallel with the old system to check on customer and employee problems and reactions. Documentation is completed, accurate, and usable. Most importantly, the system meets or exceeds the business requirement as stated at the end of the requirements definition phase, and each of the quality attributes meets the criteria established for successful business operation.

In addition to the business manager, participants to delivery and acceptance include the following:

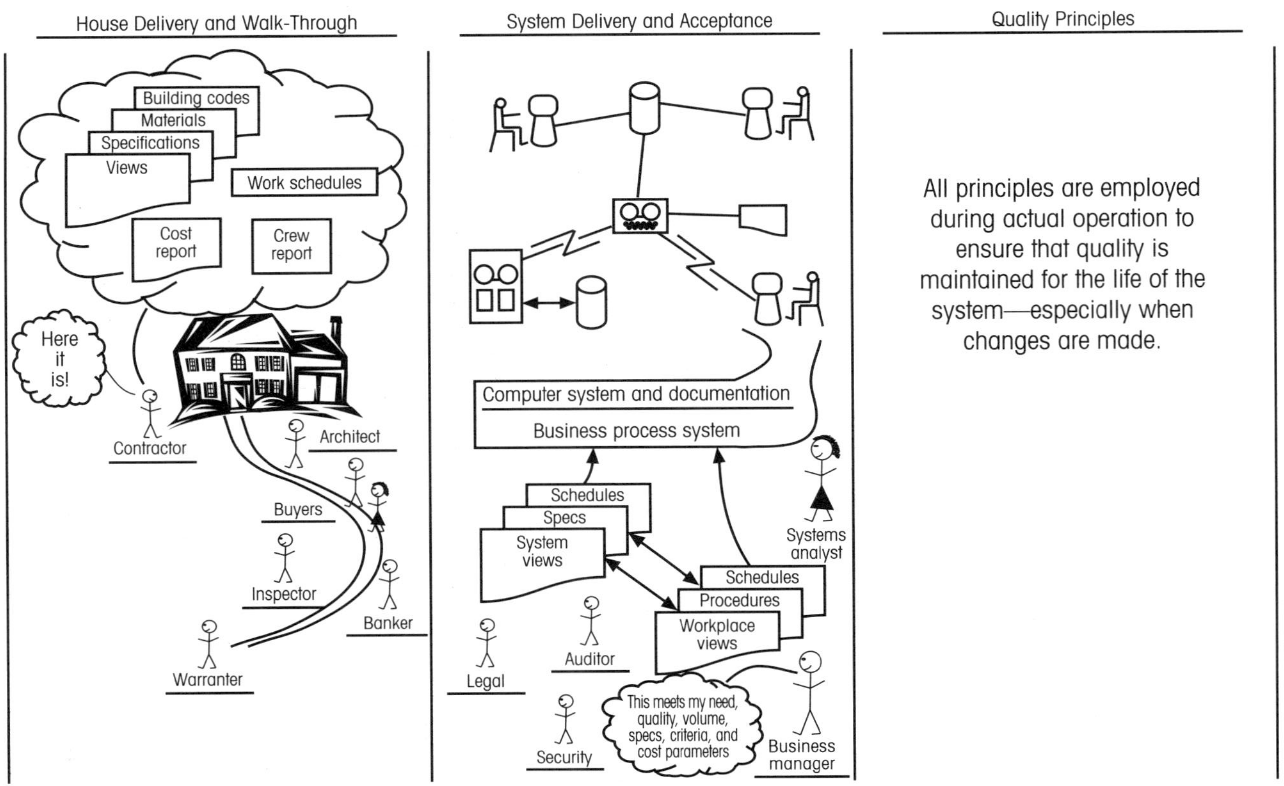

Figure 9.1. Finally—delivery!

- Legal department
- Internal and external auditor
- Security officer
- Financial officer
- Business manager

Each of these participants has a fiduciary or legal responsibility, or both. Each is responsible to the business owner for systems that operate within the guidelines that govern his or her area of professional expertise. All participants are asked to certify that the system, to the best of their knowledge and judgment, will not subject the business to unacceptable risk. They are acting as the building inspectors of the technical/manual system. They assure executive management that the system, as delivered, meets specification and is soundly constructed.

In a practical sense, for a small business, the manager may fufill many of these roles. In a large company separate organizational departments may participate in the final acceptance tests of the system. In either case, it is important to ensure that these interested groups are actively involved and not just passively nodding their heads during some final briefing conducted by the contractor or in-house developer. Of course, if the methods presented in this book have been followed, these interested participants will have been involved from the very start of requirements definition and are now merely determining whether their previously stated requirements are met by the delivered system and are working effectively.

Of course, the business managers' principal concern is the improved processing of the business function that IT was suppose to enhance. In making this operational determination, managers will also return to the statement of requirements generated during the definition phase and use the measures of quality and performance that were determined at that time to judge the acceptability of the finished system.

Historically, the interests of most organizational participants were not met and the subsequent risk to the business had to be accepted; or a series of potentially disruptive and expensive modifications were undertaken to fix the system after it had become operational. This no longer need be the case if the development approach outlined in this book is followed.

It may take some persuasion to obtain the involvement of some organizational groups, but the architect/analyst should be able to assist in this task by educating reluctant participants to the risks involved and the implications of their noninvolvement. No business manager should attempt any sort of automation without the full support and participation of appropriate corporate oversight groups.

Business managers or systems developers should no longer be willing, as in the past, to singly accept the blame for nonquality systems. IT systems support the business as a whole, and each organizational element representing the various management disciplines is responsible for ensuring the acceptability of the uses and applications of technology. If poor quality systems and services prevail, the blame cannot be singly placed at any one doorstep.

Considerations for Successful Operations and Maintenance

This concluding discussion deals with issues affecting successful long-term operation and maintenance of the IT system, after delivery and acceptance. Beginning to address these issues at this phase of development is inadequate! These are issues that should have been contemplated during each previous phase and were of special concern during alternatives analysis when feasibility factors were examined in detail. The issues are discussed here for ease of presentation and for the purpose of emphasizing their importance. Successful system operation and maintenance depends on two major factors: the existence of a stable working environment for both operators and maintenance personnel; and a successful service relationship, if maintenance is done under contract.

Stable Operations Environment

After system delivery and acceptance, all hardware, software, and documentation required for smooth day-to-day operations should be present. The challenge facing both technical and business managers is to maintain, over time, the same level of operational and environmental integrity as existed at the time of final system acceptance. This means that any change to the system, the operational environment, or the workplace must be handled in a disciplined manner.

In order to ensure system level integrity, for any proposed change, it is always necessary to perform an *impact analysis* on the operational system. Changes can affect the technical part of the system or workplace procedures, or both. Changes can result from problems identified and corrected or from improvements and enhancements added to increase system capabilities and efficiencies. By their very nature, changes put the stability and integrity of the current operational system at risk. For this reason, those responsible for system operation and maintenance must have a clearly defined and enforced process for introducing changes to the system.

A *change control procedure* is essential to prevent the operating environment from deteriorating. This process of change control demands the same degree of detailed analysis and test as was required during initial systems development. The same analytic steps must be followed and completed in the same sequence. A change control procedure should incorporate the same analytic thought processes that were used during original development—but in an abbreviated and accelerated form. For this to be possible, systems documentation must be current and accurate, and enforcement of the change process itself must be continually required by business managers.

Change control cannot be forgotten or ignored, otherwise system integrity and stability are compromised and all previous efforts to develop quality systems are negated. Uncontrolled and untested changes can destroy—overnight—months and even years of disciplined quality-oriented development.

Change Control and the Philosophy of Continuous Improvement

QM advocates generally ascribe to the concept of continuous improvement the power to institutionalize quality into the business' long-term management practices. It is the implementation of the check-improve-do methodology—a variation of Shewhart's plan-do-check-act cycle—that gives substantial hope that quality will become more than a one-time facilitated event. The check-improve-do approach is proposed here as consistent with traditional IT configuration management and change control procedures.

The check-improve-do sequence is central to both the change control procedure and to efforts to continuously improve the automated system. Figure 9.2 depicts the sequence in which the process is performed and lists triggering inputs and possible resultant outputs. The sequence is initiated at the *check* step, when measurements are made for system effectiveness and customer satisfaction. When problems or suggestions for improvement are encountered, the process moves to the *improve* step, where analysis and design for system modifications take place. During the improve step, the early phases of the SDP are revisited and the tests of feasibility are again performed. Designs for implementation are evaluated, and planning for an orderly implementation takes place. Once planned, actions are identified and schedules and resources are available. Then the *do* step begins. *Do* constitutes the same activities as the construction and integration phases of the SDP. Finally, the system changes are tested, documented, accepted, and put into operation.

The process itself acts on the system's components at the center of Figure 9.2. The check-improve-do steps serve as an abbreviated systems development process, where the same level of disciplined analytic thought is required as when the system was originally developed, and the same intensity of review and testing is performed. It is imperative that each

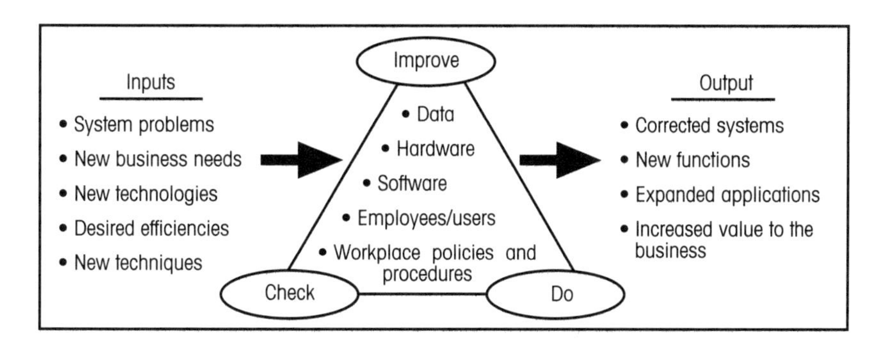

Figure 9.2. Check-improve-do steps.

circuit of the check-improve-do cycle proceed from an accurately documented baseline of the system, in its current configuration. For this, system operations management must maintain accurate configuration data and up-to-date documentation of all components comprising the configuration. In the early stages of system life this may seem a simple task, but as the system evolves and matures, this can pose major problems. Contemporary solutions to configuration management problems include the use of automated tools to identify, track, and control the testing and release of operational workplace environment changes. The importance of maintaining integrity and currency of existing system documentation cannot be overemphasized. Failure of the information systems provider (in-house or contractor) to provide such baseline stability can lead to rapid system deterioration and excessively high maintenance costs—if, in fact, maintenance is even possible.

Essentials for Successful Maintenance

Whether maintenance support is an in-house activity or accomplished under contract, attention to the following essentials will help keep it responsive and cost-effective.

1. Develop and refine a solid understanding of the system's maintenance needs. Downtime and service interruption record keeping is necessary to identify maintenance levels and to negotiate fee rates at contract renewal time. Trouble call turnaround, pricing, spare parts, alternate sources of supply, and any unique demands need to be documented.

2. Completely understand warranties and the business' rights under the contract. Obtain qualified legal assistance, as needed.

3. Make sure the maintenance provider (in-house or contractor) has the expertise and reputation required to meet requirements. Check references just as when selecting an information systems and software supplier.

4. Do not let price drive the maintenance support decision. Levels of expertise, scheduled hours of maintenance, response time for off-schedule maintenance and trouble calls, and charges for spare parts and depot activities should all be weighed against the operational requirements for sup-

port of the business function. The maintenance support agreement should be based on the best value to the business over the long haul.

5. Communication between the business and the systems maintenance provider is of great importance. Review and feedback are essential.

6. Bigger is not always better! Some suppliers, by concentrating on a few products, possess a special advantage over big maintenance houses. Bigger may be an advantage, however, when multiple vendor equipments constitute the systems' configuration and complex diagnostics and solution integration are needed. Do not split maintenance between providers unless absolutely necessary. Finger-pointing will result.

7. Think and act for the long term. Each installation and system configuration creates, over time, a unique picture of problems and implemented solutions. This becomes a prime input to future problem diagnosis as a system and configuration matures. It is desirable to manage with an available history of system components, changes, and maintenance. This is not possible if unnecessary changes in maintenance providers are experienced. It is important to view the maintenance provider as a key element to the overall long-term success of the operation, and any decisions to change maintenance provider should take this factor into account.

8. Periodically review service quality and help set reasonable expectations for all those using the system. Establish the warranty or contract parameters prior to beginning repairs. Monitor maintenance trouble tickets and charges to identify trends in component reliability and unexpected defects and resultant downtime. Conduct periodic meetings with the maintenance provider.

9. The equipment's life can be extended by attention to maintenance records. Determining cause for an equipment failure often uncovers environmental (that is, dust, heat, and power problems) hazards that can affect an entire configuration. Preventive maintenance must be accomplished according to a schedule.

Quality Principles Employed

Improving quality is a never-ending journey that focuses on the processes used to produce goods and deliver services. The QM principles have been employed throughout each phase of the system development project, and finally, because of a conscientious adherence to these principles, business managers are rewarded with a system that contributes value to the business process, since it works properly and contributes to improved productivity or customer service.

As discussed in this chapter, however, the battle for quality is a day-to-day struggle to maintain an operational environment where quality is not degraded and where continuous quality improvements can take place. This means that the QM principles need to be incorporated into the philosophies and practices of overall business operations. The partnership, between business managers and technologists, which was so important to obtaining a valued system or service, must now be expanded to create a TQM organization.

If the business has not yet explored concepts of TQM, now is the time to do so! If these concepts were introduced to the company some time ago, now is the time to evaluate progress and take any necessary resuscitation steps to get back on track. The continuing operational value and future quality of IT systems and subsequent business services depend on the extent and degree of organizational quality awareness and commitment to excellence.

The major theme presented throughout this book has centered on the essential and proactive involvement of business managers to set the course for the quality and value-added use of technology. If automation is to make its greatest contribution it must be viewed as a means to an end—not an end to itself. Keeping the technology of information processing in its appropriately subordinate role and requiring that its processes and output be of high quality, mean that the criteria, by which these processes and outputs are judged, be derived from a clear and concise understanding of what constitutes quality. There is no magic by which IT, in and of itself, can improve the quality of anything. It is only within the context of the overall business process that sufficient specifications can be articulated to direct a successful and value-added use of technology. This general context can only come through management's adoption of quality principles and practices for the entire enterprise. This adoption creates an environment whereby the considerable effort required to maintain information system quality is seen as not only desirable, but also necessary.

Final Thoughts

In the years ahead, look for the IT industry to become more customer-oriented by establishing certification and accreditation schemes where companies seek a competitive advantage by attaining documented levels of quality and service excellence and advertising this fact. This is occurring now in the software development arena where companies are pursuing the Software Engineering Institute's Capability Maturity Matrix Program, and where improvements are sought by using the ISO guideline 9000-3. As long as these and similar efforts refrain from becoming just bureaucratic exercises, they will provide nontechnical managers with future first-cut review mechanisms when seeking IT support.

There will, however, never be a substitute for knowing requirements, checking references, and developing IT support systems consistent with an approach that keeps automation in its appropriate subordinate role.

APPENDIX

Business Managers' Systems Development Summary Guide

The following guide summarizes the major activities observed of an IT project, which is following sound system development practices and which employs the principles of quality management. The questions presented in this guide can be used by business managers to ensure that a project's plan of action follows recommended practice. It can be used to check activities of an ongoing development, especially for a new manager joining a project. Finally, this guide can be used to determine the degree to which development activities have been documented. This last element, documentation, can prove critical to an attempt to bring, or defend against, legal action should system failure result in damage to a business or any of its customers.

Involve All Stakeholders

- Who, from your business processing areas, participated in the definition of requirements for the system/software?
- Were all business activities to be impacted by the system represented?
- Are the requirements documented?

Depending on the nature and complexity of the business application, there are many stakeholders who should have an operational, legal, audit, security, management, and customer relations interest in the system/software. They must participate in the definition of requirements and concur with those requirements if the developer is to know what to design, program, test, and deliver.

State All Requirements

- Were the attributes of quality and performance defined as a set of specifications precisely describing the requirement of the system/software?
- Did the *stakeholders* reach consensus concerning how satisfaction of each attribute would be measured?
- Were these attributes documented?
- Were criteria for measuring success identified?

Without a clear and concise understanding of how requirements of the system/software are measured by the stakeholders and customers, the developer does not have the information necessary to design and construct the system/software. Without such acceptance data, the developer has no realistic criteria against which to test the design of the system or the program code.

Perform Alternatives Analysis

- Were alternative ways of meeting the requirements proposed?
- Did these proposals encompass both the technical and workplace aspects of a system?
- Were these proposals subjected to the tests of feasibility; that is, technical, operational, and economic?
- Was the most feasible alternative proposed and selected? If not, why not?
- Are these proposals, tests of feasibility, and recommendations documented?

Ensure Security Controls

- How were the adequacy of security and audit controls for this type of application determined?
- Are they considered sufficient by industry practice or are they required by standards governing functions of the business (for example, financial or accounting guidelines, or those of government regulators such as the Food and Drug Administration)?
- Is this analysis and decision process documented?

Determine Validation, Verification, and Test Sufficiency

- How was the adequacy of validation, verification, and test activities for the project determined?
- Was the degree of testing considered appropriate by industry practice for similar systems/software?
- Is this thought process documented?

The answers to these questions require the performance of some type of risk analysis. Was a risk analysis conducted, taking into account the critical nature of the application, the sensitivity of information, and the susceptibility of the application to possible fraud and abuse? Did the stakeholders have input to the risk analysis, and were computer security and internal control specialists involved in determining appropriate controls, given the identified weaknesses and threats to the system? An inability to show evidence of this type of preventive thinking could make it difficult to claim that a reasonable approach was taken to systems design and development.

Use a Systems Development Process (SDP)

- What SDP is being followed during this project?
- Do the analysts and programmers on the project appear to be trained in the SDP?
- Are they held responsible for following the sequence of development steps laid out by the SDP?

- Are the SDP work products documented?

Conduct SDP Reviews

- Did the SDP incorporate periodic review points, where work on the project was validated against requirements for the system/software?
- Were these reviews actually conducted?
- Did the stakeholders participate in the review?
- When errors, omissions, or changes were found and corrections made, were they reflected in the systems' documentation?
- Can the documentation be produced?

Determine Technical Correctness During Development

- Does management of the system/software effort require the periodic verification for technical correctness and to ensure that sound design and programming practices are followed?
- As soon as possible, are work products reviewed against the predetermined acceptance criteria that has been established?

It is important that the project be well supervised. The project review points, where progress against requirements and the plan is examined to determine appropriateness and correctness of preceding work products, are integral parts of all SDPs. Evidence of having conducted these reviews is essential to claiming that a reasonable approach has been taken during the development effort.

Provide for Independent Quality Reviews

- Was there a quality assurance function operating during development of this system/software?
- Was quality assurance involved during the early phases of development to ensure that all attributes of a quality software system were addressed?

- What national or international standards (such as ISO 9000-3) constituted the benchmark for quality?
- Were the personnel responsible for the quality assurance function independent of the development team and management structure?
- Did any external review take place while the system/software was under development?
- Can you find documentary proof that quality assurance project reviews were performed?

Retaining Continuity During the Project

- How was the continuity of the development team maintained?
- As work progressed, how was knowledge of the design requirements and the testing and acceptance criteria passed from one team member to another?
- On large projects, how were the many ongoing development activities coordinated and controlled?
- Can this process be described to you and does it work?

Again, the need to demonstrate sufficient management control over the project is essential to the claim that reasonable care was exercised. The problems associated with configuration management, especially on large projects, must be overcome if a quality product is to be delivered.

Manage Change to Requirements

- As requirements change or were refined and modified, how were they managed to ensure that unexpected adverse impacts did not affect the software or system under development?
- What policies and procedures existed to prevent programmers from making changes without proper analysis and testing?

System/software projects are very difficult to manage. Most SDPs and project management methods provide techniques for disciplined control of the development effort. All too often, however, they are not utilized and programmers/analysts are given too much latitude to determine what they will and will not do on a project. To show that reasonable care was exercised, it must be clear that the analysts and programmers were under management control.

Document Testing Efforts

- Did the development schedule allot sufficient time for system/software testing?
- Were employees, knowledgeable in testing, asked to provide estimates for this project?
- Was testing done manually or were automated testing tools employed?
- Does documentation concerning the testing program for this project exist?

Manage Testing

- How was the testing program managed for this project?
- What national or international standards were used to guide the testing?
- Were any industry-specific requirements used to direct the testing effort?
- Where is the evidence that those standards or unique requirements were satisfied?

Adequate and sufficient testing form the major element of a defense against any legal challenge. For example, under strict liability law, liability for injuries may be imposed without any showing of fault. In some cases, if a product is made in a defective manner and causes injury, the manufacturer is liable without the showing of any fault whatsoever.

While the existence of bugs and flaws in software and systems are accepted by unknowing customers as the way things are, professional developers are required, as experts, to do whatever is necessary to deliver quality software and systems, given the state of the software engineering art and the criticality of the application for which the software is developed. This is why the risk analysis was important. Highly critical applications require more stringent testing than do mundane and less sensitive applications.

Developers must be able to show that, as experts, sufficient time was allotted to do a thorough job of testing. Any inappropriate pressure to curtail or reduce test time should be carefully documented and should show that short cuts were cautioned against.

Manage Document Changes During Testing

- As testing progressed, how were errors, omissions, and required corrective changes managed?
- Has all preceding system/software documentation been modified to reflect such changes?
- Do test plans and test data reflect such changes?
- Were all changes during testing and subsequent reprogramming analyzed for security and audit implications?
- Does documentary evidence exist?

Keep Documentation Current

- Was system/software documentation kept current throughout the development effort and not just fabricated near the end of the project?
- If continuing support for the system/software was provided, is documentation maintained reflecting all modifications occurring since final delivery?
- Is configuration management used to control maintenance testing and release of software into production?

Avoid Shortcuts

- Were any corners cut in either testing or in documentation in order to get the code operational before it was ready?
- Can this be proven?

Establish Review Points

- Can customer acceptance of the system/software after each major systems development (that is, phase) review point and after each final test be shown?

Identify Insurance Needs

- What insurance does the business carry for protection against loss from system/software failure?
- Does this insurance protect against a liability suit from customers?

Almost every basic general liability insurance policy for a business excludes coverage if a company has failed to perform its professional duties. For that sort of coverage, a company must have an errors-and-omissions clause in its liability insurance policy, which few insurers will underwrite.

Get Value for Your IT Dollars

- What can you do to give top corporate management assurance that its technology dollars will result in quality systems?

References and Additional Reading

References

Crosby, P. B. 1979. *Quality is free*. New York: McGraw-Hill.

Crouch, J. M. 1992. *An ounce of application is worth a ton of abstraction.* Greensboro, N.C.: LEADS Corporation.

Drucker, P. 1992. *Managing for the future*. New York: Truman Talley Books.

Department of Trade and Industry (DTI). 1986. *Profiting from office automation: Office automation pilots.* London: Department of Trade and Industry.

Eason, K. 1988. *Information technology and organizational change*. London: Taylor and Francis.

Gibbs, W. 1994. Software's chronic crisis. *Scientific American* (September): 86.

Kindel, S. 1993. World without end. *Financial World*, 9 November, 44.

King, J. 1992. Executive report: No safety in numbers. *Computer World*, 30 March, 85–86.

Lamb, J. 1988. Computer crashes and the stranded traveler—Air traffic control in Britain. *New Scientist,* 8 September, 65.

Mowshowitz, A. 1976. *The conquest on will: Information processing in human affairs*. Reading, Mass.: Addison-Wesley.

Neumann, P. G. 1985. A comment on SEN's anthologized tales of woe. *Software Engineering Notes* 10, no. 2: 6.

———. 1988. Risks to the public in computer and related systems. *Software Engineering Notes* 10, no. 1: 9.

New York Times. 1986. Science Times section, 29 July.

Rosenthal, D., and V. A. Jategaonkan. 1995. Wanted: Qualified professionals. *Information Systems Management* (spring): 27.

Wroe, B. 1986. Contractors and computers: Why systems succeed or fail. Ph.D. diss., Loughborough University of Technology.

Zachman, J. 1987. A framework for information systems architecture. *IBM Systems Journal* 26, no. 3 (publication no. G 321-0087-00).

Zonana, V. E. 1987. $23 million computer snafu adds to B of A's troubles. *Los Angeles Times*, 24 July.

Program errors halt hospital computer works. 1989. *Los Angeles Times*, 20 September, p. 23.

Additional Reading

Baskerville, Richard. 1988. *Designing information systems security*. Chichester, U.K.: John Wiley & Sons.

Beizer, Boris. 1988. *The frozen keyboard: Living with bad software*. Blue Ridge Summit, Pa.: TAB Books.

Birrel, N. D., and M.A. Ould. 1985. *A practical handbook for software development*. Cambridge, U.K.: Cambridge University Press.

Boehm, Barry W. 1981. *Software engineering economics*. Englewood Cliffs, N.J.: Prentice Hall.

———. 1989. *Software risk management*. Washington, D.C.: IEEE Computer Society Press.

Boehm, B. W., J. T. Brown, H. Kaspar, M. Lipow, G. J. MacLeod, and M. J. Merritt. 1978. *The characteristics of software quality*. North-Holland.

Carzo, Rocco, and Yanouzas, John. 1967. *Formal qrganization: A systems approach*. Homewood, Ill.: Irwin-Dorsey.

Charette, Robert N. 1990. *Applications strategies for risk analysis.* New York: McGraw-Hill.

Cotterman, William, and James Senn. 1992. *Challenges and strategies for research in systems development.* Chichester, U.K.: John Wiley & Sons.

Covey, Stephen R 1989. *The 7 habits of highly effective people.* New York: Simon & Schuster.

Crouch, J. Michael. 1993. *An ounce of application is worth a ton of abstraction.* Greensboro, N.C.: LEADS Corporation.

DeMarco, Tom, and Timothy Lister. 1987. *Peopleware: Productive projects and teams.* New York: Dorset House.

Dijkstra, E. W. 1981. *The science of programming.* Englewood Cliffs, N.J.: Prentice Hall.

Dobyns, Lloyd, and Clare Crawford-Mason. 1991. *Quality or else: The revolution in world business.* Boston: Houghton Mifflin.

Eason, Ken. 1988. *Information technology and organizational change.* London: Taylor & Francis.

Fagan, M. E. 1976. Design and code inspections to reduce errors in program development. Fagan. *IBM Systems Journal* 15, no. 3:182-211.

Heider, John. 1985. *The Tao of leadership.* New York: Bantam Books.

ISO 9000-3. 1991. *Quality management and quality assurance systems—Guidelines for the application of ISO 9001 to the development, supply and maintance of software.* Geneva, Switzerland: International Organization for Standardization.

ISO 9001. 1994. *Quality systems—Model for quality assurance in design, development, production, installation and servicing.* Geneva, Switzerland: International Organization for Standardization.

Jones, Meilir Page. 1985. *Practical project management: Restoring quality to projects and systems.* New York: Dorset House.

Mandell, Steve. 1984. *Computer, data processing and the law.* St. Paul, Minn.: West Publishing Company.

Martin. James. 1982. *Strategic data planning methodologies.* Englewood Cliffs, N.J.: Prentice Hall, Inc.

Martin, James, and Carma McClure.1985. *Structured techniques for computing.* Englewood Cliffs, N.J.: Prentice Hall.

Mayhew, P. J., C. J. Worsley, and P. A. Dearnley. 1989. Control of software prototyping process: Change classification approach. *Information and Software Technology* 31, no. 2:59-66.

McCabe, T. J., and G. G. Schulmeyer. 1985. System testing aided by structured analysis: A practical experience. *IEEE Transactions on Software Engineering* SE-11, no. 9:917-921.

Naisbitt, John, and Patricia Aburdene. 1985. *Re-inventing the corporation.* New York: Warner Books.

Oncken, W., Jr. 1984. *Managing management time.* Englewood Cliffs, N.J.: Prentice Hall.

Optner, Stanford L. 1968. *Systems analysis for business management.* Englewood Cliffs, N.J.: Prentice Hall.

Ould, Martyn A. 1990. *Strategies for software engineering: The management of risk and quality.* New York: John Wiley & Sons.

Ould, M. A., and C. Unwin, eds. 1987. *Testing in software development.* BCS Monographs in Informatics. Cambridge, U.K.: Cambridge University Press.

Perry, William. 1990. *A standard for testing application software.* Boston: Auerbach Publishers.

Peters, Thomas, and Robert Waterman. 1982. *In search of excellence.* New York: Harper & Row.

Schindler, Max. 1990. *Computer-aided software design.* New York: John Wiley & Sons.

Sherer, Susan A. 1992. *Software failure risk: Measurement and management.* New York: Plenum Press.

Stallings, William. 1994. *Data and computer communications*. 4th ed. New York: Macmillan.

Townsend, Robert. 1984. *Further up the organization*. New York: Harper and Row.

Tucker, Robert B. 1991. *Managing the future*. New York: Berkley Books.

Walton, Mary. 1992. *The Deming management method*. New York: Perigee Books.

Whitten, Jeffrey L., Lonnie D. Bentley, and Victor M. Barlow. 1989. *Systems analysis and design methods*. Homewood, Ill.:

Irwin.Yourdon, E. 1979. *Structured walkthroughs*. New York: Yourdon Press.

Index